STAR WARS™
DARTH VADER™
SITH LORD

By Jason Fry

Illustrated by Randy Martinez and Rick Burchett

SCHOLASTIC INC.

The publisher does not have any control over and does not assume any responsibility for author or third-party websites or their content.

No part of this publication may be reproduced, stored in a retrieval system, or transmitted in any form or by any means, electronic, mechanical, photocopying, recording, or otherwise, without written permission of the publisher. For information regarding permission, write to Scholastic Inc., Attention: Permissions Department, 557 Broadway, New York, NY 10012.

This book is a work of fiction. Names, characters, places, and incidents are either the product of the author's imagination or are used fictitiously, and any resemblance to actual persons, living or dead, business establishments, events, or locales is entirely coincidental.

ISBN 978-1-338-02982-6

10 9 8 7 6 5 4 3 2 1   17 18 19 20 21

Printed in the U.S.A.   40
First printing 2017

Book design by Rick DeMonico

CONTENTS

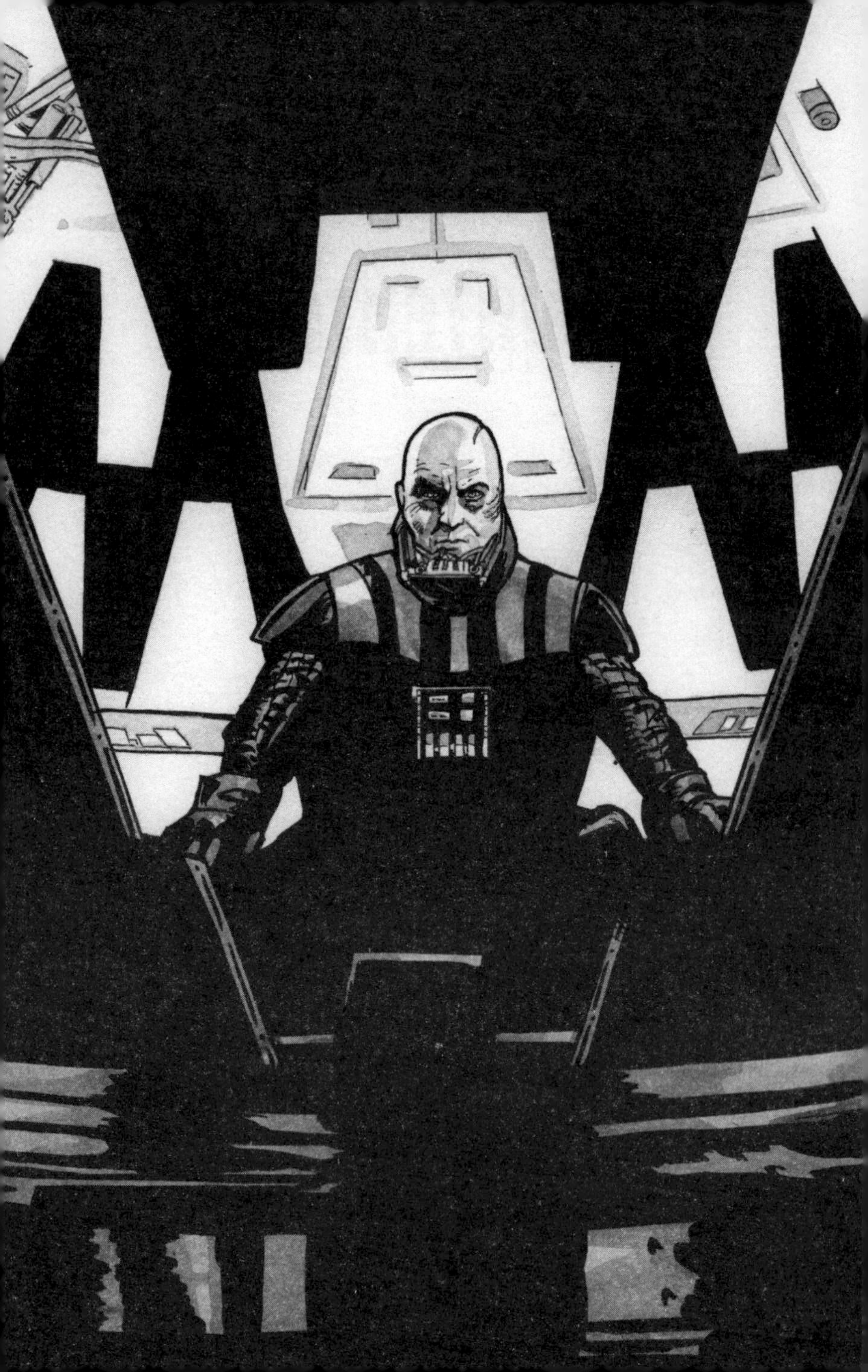

Foreword

by Darth Vader

EXHIBIT: RECOVERED HOLOGRAPHIC LOG Z3-124
ORIGIN: ATRAVIS SECTOR, PATHFINDER
    OPERATIONS FILE L-227
AUTHENTICIY: TO BE DETERMINED
* FURTHER DETAILS CLASSIFIED BY NEW
    REPUBLIC INTELLIGENCE *

Once, I was Anakin Skywalker.

Anakin Skywalker was a weak and sentimental slave. He grew into a weak man who was betrayed by those he held closest—those he fought to keep safe.

The Republic betrayed me even before I was born, by allowing slavery to flourish in the Outer Rim. The Jedi Order betrayed me when I was a child, leaving my mother in slavery and seeking to limit my power because of jealousy and fear. The worthless peasants who took in my mother betrayed both of us by allowing her to be captured, tormented, and then killed.

But the Jedi betrayed all of us—my apprentice, myself, and, ultimately, the citizens of the galaxy that they claimed to serve.

The Jedi were cowards. They denied me the title of Jedi Master. They asked me to spy on the Supreme Chancellor of the Republic. They told me to stand aside while they tried to murder him.

And then my former master betrayed me. Too cowardly to kill me, he left me to die in agony.

But I did not die in the fires of Mustafar.

Anakin Skywalker died that day. My weak and sentimental former self was finally destroyed.

But I lived.

I lived because I had opened myself to all the Jedi tried to deny: passion and emotion, which the Jedi forbade because they confused indifference to the suffering of others with peace. From passion and emotion I gained strength and power. Those are the lessons of the Sith—the importance of struggling and striving. Anger and pain are natural and part of growth. They give you focus. They make you strong.

My Sith master Darth Sidious has betrayed me, too. But this is as it must be. The Jedi betrayed Anakin Skywalker to keep him weak; my Sith master betrays me to teach me strength.

And I am strong. My armor hides the ruined body of Anakin Skywalker. But to the Force we are not such crude matter. The fires of Mustafar purified me, and in the Force I burn brightly.

Anakin Skywalker is dead. But Darth Vader is alive.

Friends, Foes, and Family

Shmi Skywalker

Anakin's mother tries to give her son a normal life even though they are slaves. She still wonders about Anakin's mysterious birth.

Qui-Gon Jinn

A maverick Jedi, Qui-Gon believes Anakin is the Chosen One of ancient Jedi prophecy, and thinks it's the will of the Force for the boy to train as a Jedi.

Padmé Amidala

When Anakin meets Padmé, she is the queen of the planet Naboo. They later fall in love, but their secret marriage is destined to end in tragedy.

Obi-Wan Kenobi

Obi-Wan trains Anakin after his master Qui-Gon Jinn's death. The two become close friends but will ultimately wind up enemies—to Obi-Wan's lasting sorrow.

Yoda

The Grand Master of the Jedi Order, Yoda has grave doubts about whether it is wise to train Anakin as a Jedi, but he tries to help the boy master his emotions.

Supreme Chancellor Palpatine

As leader of the Republic, Palpatine becomes Anakin's mentor. But he is secretly the Sith Lord Darth Sidious. He plots to twist Anakin's loyalties away from the Jedi.

Count Dooku

The political leader of the Separatists and Sidious's apprentice, Dooku bests Anakin in a lightsaber duel following the Battle of Geonosis. But the two will meet again.

Ahsoka Tano

Yoda sends this brash young Togruta to be Anakin's Padawan. Yoda hopes teaching Ahsoka will help Anakin let go of emotional attachments that cloud his judgment.

Luke Skywalker

Anakin's secret son, Luke is raised on Tatooine and taught the ways of the Force by Obi-Wan—who also tells him that Darth Vader killed his father.

Leia Organa

Luke's twin sister, Leia, is raised by adoptive parents on Alderaan and becomes a rebel leader. Darth Vader hunts her down because she stole the Death Star plans, but never suspects she is his daughter.

Chronology

The son of Shmi Skywalker, Anakin is born into slavery in the Outer Rim.

When the Jedi Master Qui-Gon Jinn is stranded on Tatooine, he meets Anakin. Qui-Gon believes Anakin is the Chosen One, foretold by ancient Jedi prophecy.

Qui-Gon makes a wager that earns Anakin his freedom, but Anakin has to leave his mother behind when he chooses to go with Qui-Gon.

A decade later, Anakin meets Padmé again. The two fall in love. But Anakin has nightmares that his mother is in danger. He and Padmé return to Tatooine to find her.

Anakin discovers Shmi near death as a captive of the Tusken Raiders. Overcome by anger and pain, he slaughters the Tuskens.

Anakin duels the Separatist leader Count Dooku, who severs the young Jedi's lower arm.

Ahsoka leaves the Jedi Order. Anakin blames his fellow Jedi for betraying his Padawan's trust.

Anakin and Obi-Wan rescue Supreme Chancellor Palpatine from General Grievous, with Anakin defeating Count Dooku and then killing him.

Padmé tells Anakin she's pregnant—and he begins having nightmares that she will die in childbirth.

On Coruscant, the galactic capital, the Jedi Council refuses to let Qui-Gon train Anakin as a Jedi because the boy is too old.

Anakin saves the people of Naboo—Padmé's homeworld—by blowing up the Trade Federation's Droid Control Ship.

After Qui-Gon's death, the Council agrees that Obi-Wan Kenobi, Qui-Gon's apprentice, may train Anakin.

Anakin secretly marries Padmé on Naboo.

Anakin becomes a general in the Clone Wars, fighting heroically on many worlds as his Force powers grow.

Yoda assigns Anakin a Padawan, Ahsoka Tano, in an effort to teach the young Jedi the importance of abandoning his emotional attachments.

Palpatine tells Anakin that he is actually the Sith Lord Darth Sidious, and promises to share with Anakin secret lore that could save Padmé's life.

When the Jedi try to arrest Palpatine, Anakin helps kill Mace Windu. He becomes Sidious's Sith apprentice, and is given the name Darth Vader.

To gain strength in the dark side of the Force, Vader marches on the Jedi Temple and kills many of the Jedi.

Obi-Wan and Padmé confront Vader on Mustafar. Thinking his wife has betrayed him, Vader strangles her with the Force, leaving her unconscious.

Vader and Obi-Wan duel. Obi-Wan defeats Vader and leaves him for dead, but Sidious rescues his apprentice. His ruined body is encased in black armor. Sidious tells Vader that his anger killed Padmé.

Vader becomes the enforcer of the new Galactic Empire, hunting down fugitive Jedi and the Empire's enemies.

Vader discovers the rebel pilot is Luke Skywalker—the child he thought died with Padmé—and comes up with a plan to overthrow Darth Sidious.

Vader duels Luke on Cloud City, cutting off Luke's hand and revealing that he is the young Jedi's father. But Luke refuses to join Vader to fight the Emperor and escapes.

The Emperor sends Vader to Endor to supervise the construction of the second Death Star. He tells Vader that Luke will seek him out in time. Luke does so, setting up a confrontation between the young Jedi and the Sith Master and apprentice.

Vader helps Grand Moff Tarkin supervise construction of the Death Star, a destructive battle station. After rebel operatives steal the Death Star plans, Vader tracks the plans to Leia Organa, capturing her and interrogating her aboard the Death Star.

Obi-Wan Kenobi tries to rescue Leia, and duels Vader. Vader strikes down his former master, but Obi-Wan vanishes, passing into the Force.

An unknown rebel pilot with great strength in the Force destroys the Death Star, though Vader escapes in his TIE fighter.

Luke convinces Vader to turn away from evil. Vader throws the Emperor to his death to save Luke, sacrificing his own life and restoring balance to the Force.

Luke burns Vader's armor on Endor and is visited by the spirit of a redeemed Anakin Skywalker, reunited with Yoda and Obi-Wan in the Force.

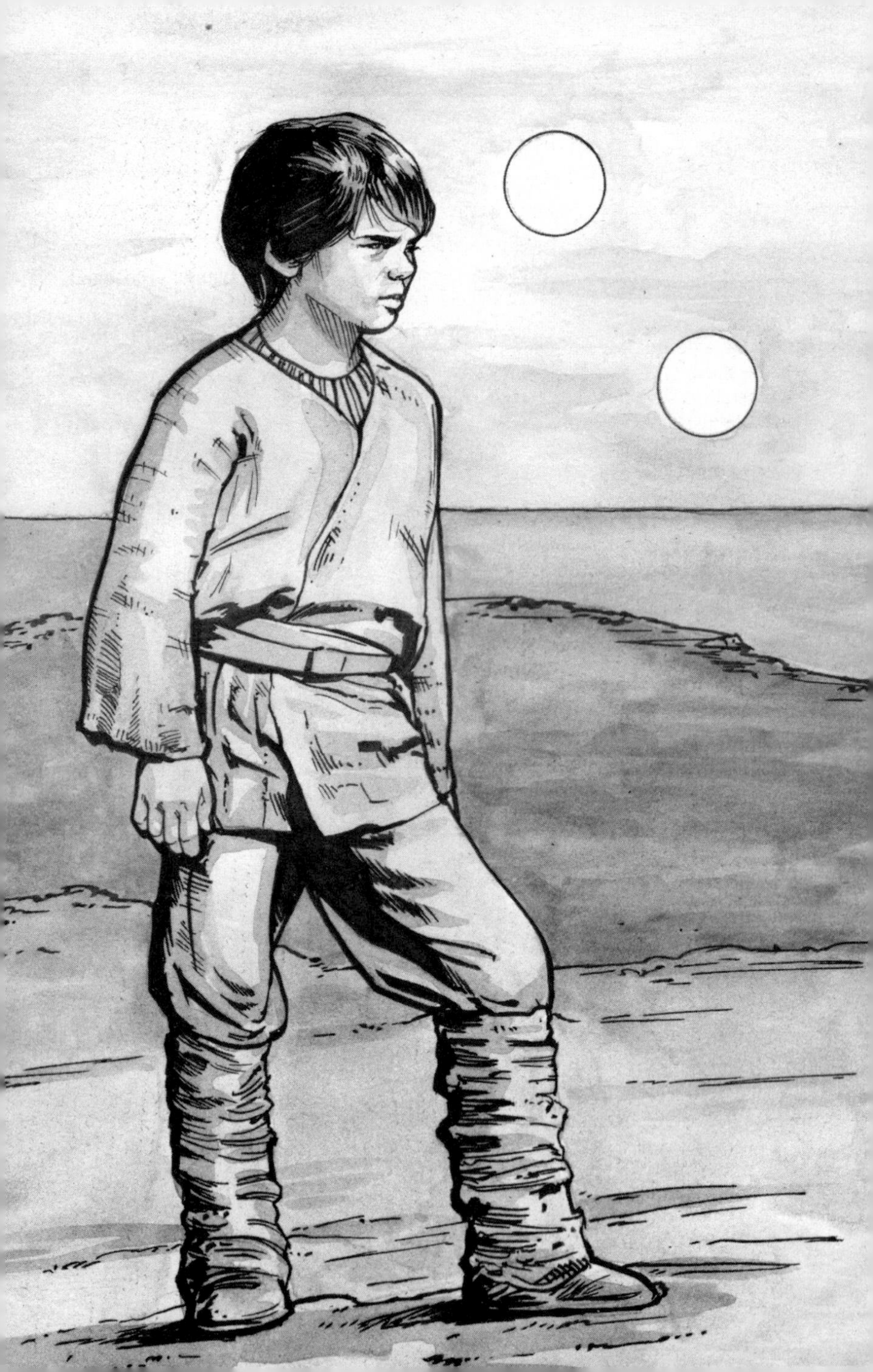

CHAPTER ONE

ENSLAVED ON TATOOINE

Years before becoming a great Jedi Knight and then falling into darkness as the evil Darth Vader, Anakin Skywalker lived a humble life as a slave on the desert planet Tatooine.

It is uncertain where Anakin was born. Some records say Anakin was born on Tatooine; other sources say Anakin and his mother, Shmi Skywalker, arrived on the remote planet of Tatooine when Anakin was very young.

Even though the Republic had outlawed slavery, Tatooine was in the galaxy's Outer Rim. On the distant planets, laws were difficult to enforce. The idea that "might makes right" was the law in these lands.

Anakin and Shmi were slaves owned by Gardulla the Hutt. They had no freedom. Anakin grew up with a transmitter implanted in his body. The transmitter allowed his master to track his whereabouts at all times. Slaves did not have any rights, and their owners could trade or sell them.

Anakin grew up without a father. Most on Tatooine assumed Anakin's father had died or been sold to some other master, breaking up their family. But the truth was much stranger.

There was no father. Shmi didn't know how she became pregnant. When she gave birth she was frightened, but was relieved when Anakin turned out to be a typical happy baby boy. Shmi kept the truth about her son's birth secret. She knew that people either wouldn't believe her or would be afraid.

Shmi tried to give Anakin the best life she could. She worked hard for her master Gardulla to ensure her son had enough to eat and a place to sleep. She almost never imagined escaping slavery, but she dreamed Anakin would be free one day. Shmi did everything she could to make sure the boy's time as a slave would have as little effect on him as possible.

When Anakin was only three, Gardulla the Hutt's habit of betting on Tatooine's podraces led to a new owner for Anakin and his mother. Gardulla lost a podracing bet to

a pudgy, winged Toydarian named Watto. The bet was for two slaves.

Watto sold droids and parts from an overstuffed junk shop in Mos Espa. He was very pleased with his new slaves. The Toydarian could tell that Shmi was excellent at cleaning and repairing equipment—she worked hard, carefully, and honestly. But Watto also had his eye on young Anakin—despite being just three years old, the boy had a knack for understanding how machines worked.

Having Watto as an owner made Anakin and Shmi's lives better in some ways. They lived in a house that was large compared to that of most slaves—Anakin and Shmi both had their own bedrooms. And Watto could be kind—he let Shmi work from the Skywalker home, and sometimes allowed Anakin to go home early when his shop had few customers.

But for slaves, life under a kind master still meant knowing you were someone else's property. Watto repeatedly warned Shmi that they would have to share their home once he bought more slaves. And if Watto fell on hard times and needed credits, he might sell Shmi or Anakin, separating mother and child. And in the lawless Outer Rim, an angry master could simply kill a slave. That made for an uncertain and frightening life.

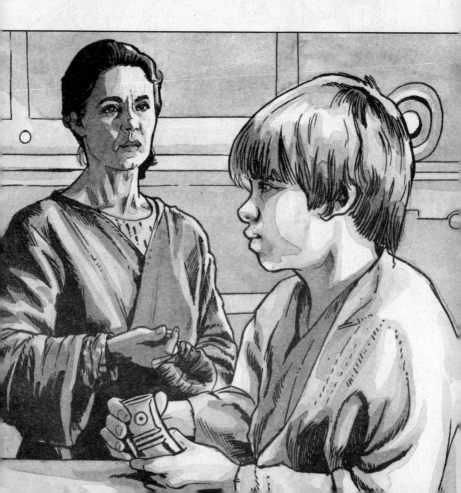

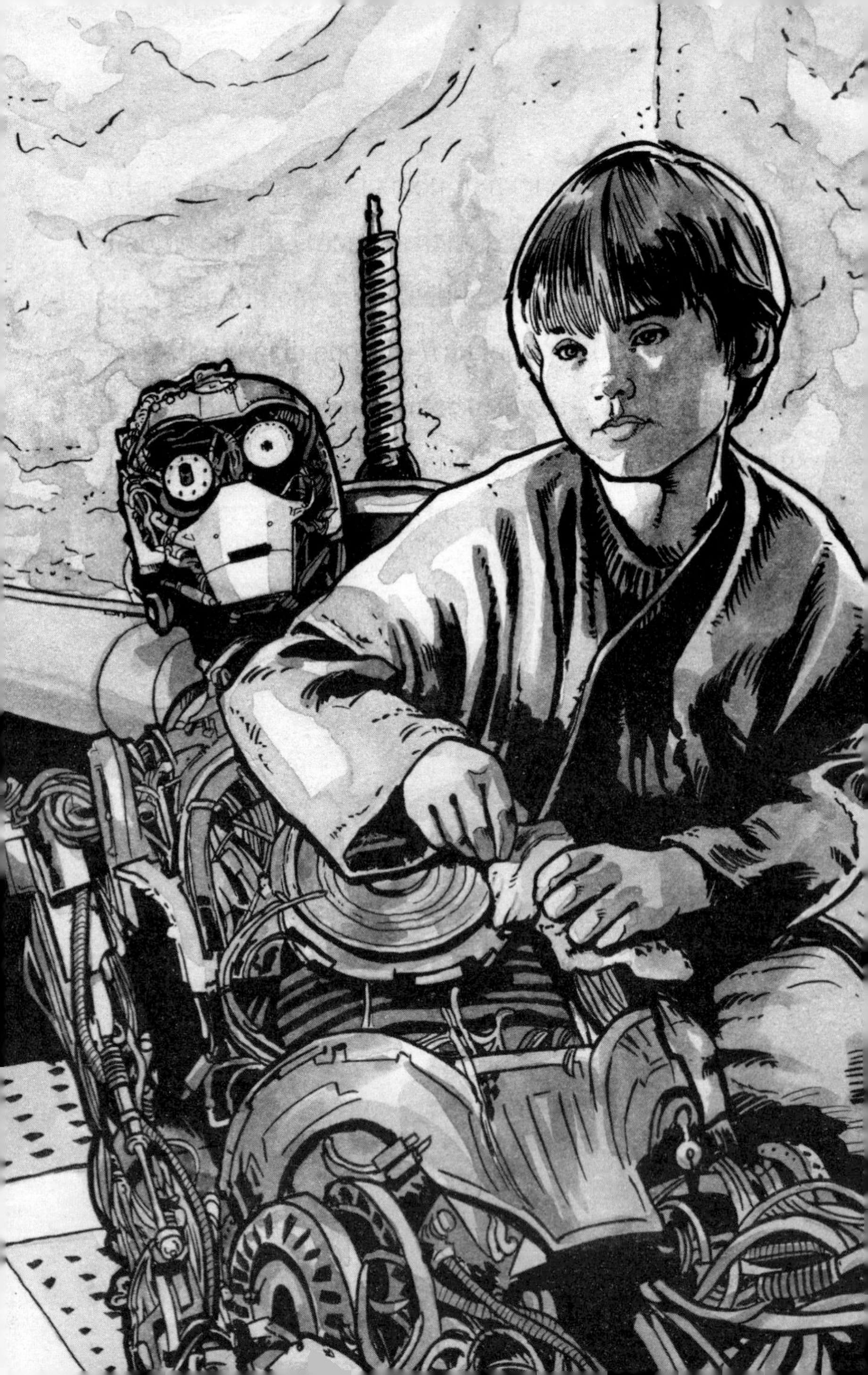

CHAPTER TWO

A NEW MASTER

Watto's shop was the perfect place for Anakin to teach himself to repair machines. It looked like any of the other junk stores in Mos Espa, but the Toydarian had an eye for a bargain and used a network of scavengers and Jawa traders to find valuable parts. Among the piles of junk, a shopper could find rare equipment no one else in Mos Espa had—equipment for which Watto charged as much as he could.

As Anakin grew older, he developed an uncanny ability for repairing items that seemed impossible to fix. He could also take parts that shouldn't go together and make them into functional machines. Sometimes they even worked better than the originals.

Watto liked Anakin—he thought most humans were clumsy and lazy, but the boy was different. He sometimes allowed Anakin to take home scrap and wrecked gear, curious to see what the boy could make from the worthless junk.

Anakin was honest when dealing with Watto's customers—he'd seen what happened to slaves who stole credits. But he sometimes helped himself to old parts Watto had set aside and apparently forgotten about, or he swapped broken parts for working ones in equipment Watto had bought but not inspected, or kept gear he found in Mos Espa's junk heaps instead of turning it over to his master. Working on his own, Anakin built a protocol droid, C-3PO, out of borrowed, scavenged, and rebuilt components. Protocol droids weren't much use on Tatooine, but Anakin imagined C-3PO could run errands and help his mother around the house once he was complete. And Anakin felt drawn

WATTO

A Toydarian junk dealer, Watto had a keen eye for equipment he could sell and a weakness for making big bets on podraces. He won Anakin and Shmi from Gardulla the Hutt, and treated his slaves better than many masters did. But his kindness was primarily about profit: Slaves who were treated well worked harder and better than abused ones.

to the wrecked droid—it was like poor Threepio needed him.

Anakin's kindness made Shmi proud. While he could get angry about being a slave, Anakin usually wanted to help others, and did so without thinking of a reward. He helped out old Jira in the marketplace, and defended his friends Kitster and Wald against slaves and free children who tried to fight them. He

approached confused travelers who might fall prey to Mos Espa's petty criminals. He also felt sorry for down-on-their-luck Jawas, injured Tusken Raiders, and even discarded protocol droids.

Shmi was less happy about Anakin's interest in podracing, which he'd picked up from Watto. The boy instinctively loved the speed of the machines, and was thrilled by the skill of the pilots and the way they seemed to laugh at the dangers of the racecourse.

Anakin dreamed of becoming a podracer pilot himself, which Watto found funny—humans were too heavy and slow to control the lightning-fast craft. But one day the Toydarian caught Anakin flying a podracer Watto had agreed to repair. Watto's anger turned to amazement when he realized the boy was handling the powerful machine with ease.

That gave Watto an idea: he could make money by sponsoring Anakin in podraces. Most podracing fans would doubt the young human's ability, so Watto could win big if he ever came in first. Watto paid the fee to

get Anakin qualified as a pilot, and acquired podracers for the boy to fly. Shmi objected, but Watto ignored her—and Anakin genuinely loved flying. Hurtling over the desert sands of Tatooine in a podracer made him feel free, if only for a moment.

Anakin didn't win his first few podraces—in fact, he didn't even finish. Sometimes the problem was his own lack of experience; other times it was Watto's junky podracers. He also fell victim to the champion podracer Sebulba, a Dug who cheated whenever he could, smashing his opponents' crafts and blasting them with hidden flame-jets. But Watto wasn't concerned. Anakin's early failures meant he'd be a long shot in betting parlors. When he finally did win, Watto would collect a huge payday.

Meanwhile, Anakin had a secret of his own. He'd salvaged junked podracer parts and was building his own craft, one he swore would be the fastest ever.

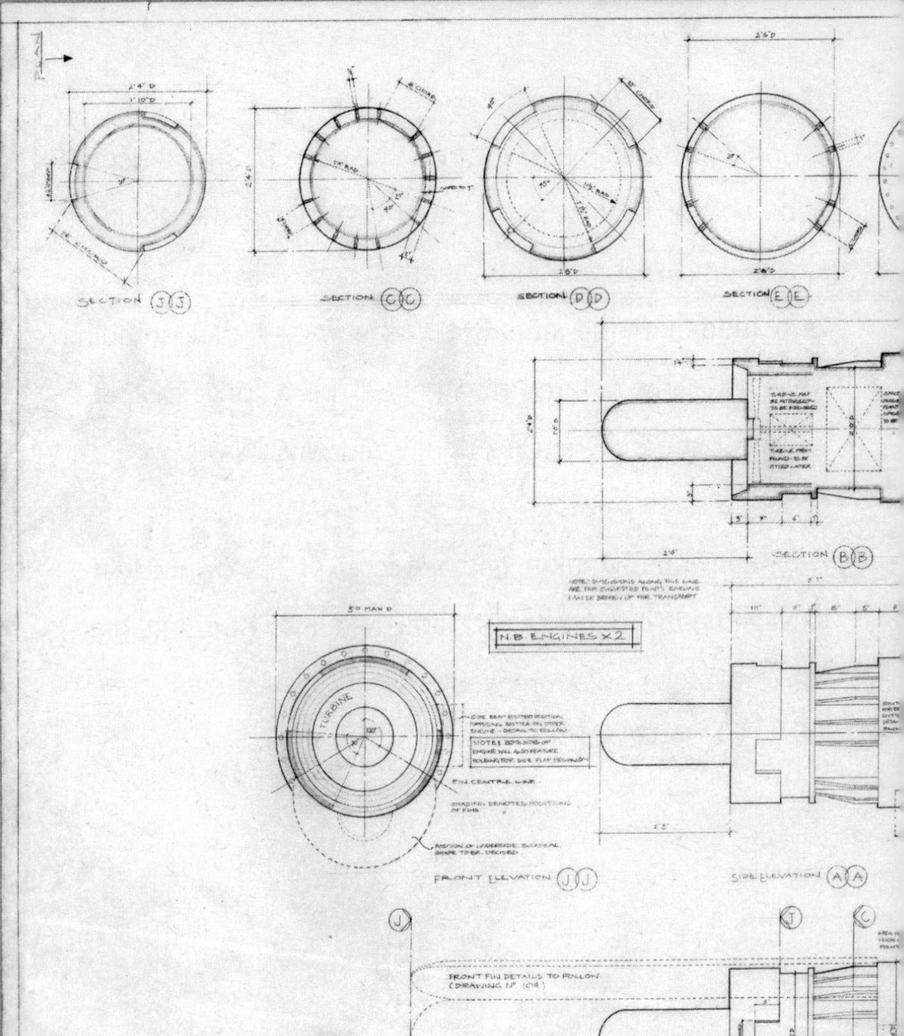
PLAN
SECTION J J
SECTION C C
SECTION D D
SECTION E E
SECTION B B
N.B. ENGINES X 2
TURBINE
FIN CENTRE LINE
FRONT ELEVATION J J
SIDE ELEVATION A A
FRONT FIN DETAILS TO FOLLOW
(DRAWING Nº 1019)
8'0" FIN LENGTH
PLAN ELEVATION

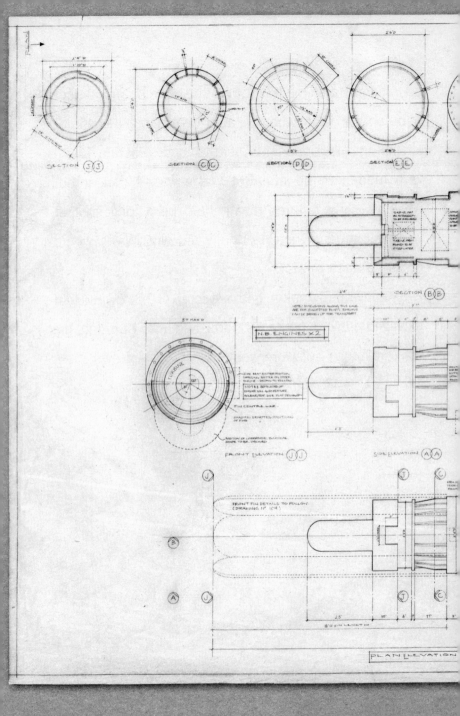

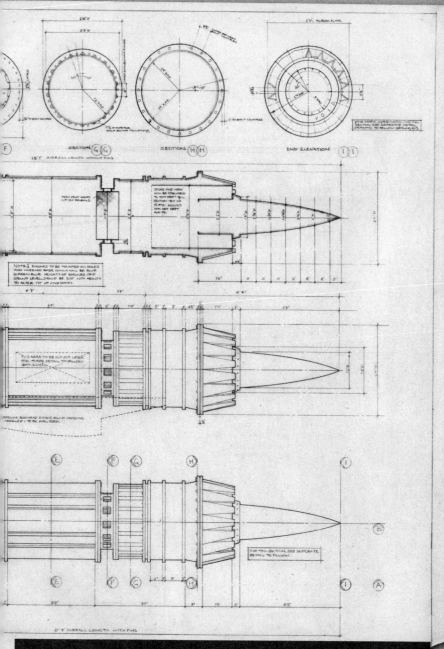

ANAKIN SECRETLY BUILT A PODRACER OF HIS OWN OUT
OF SALVAGED COMPONENTS.

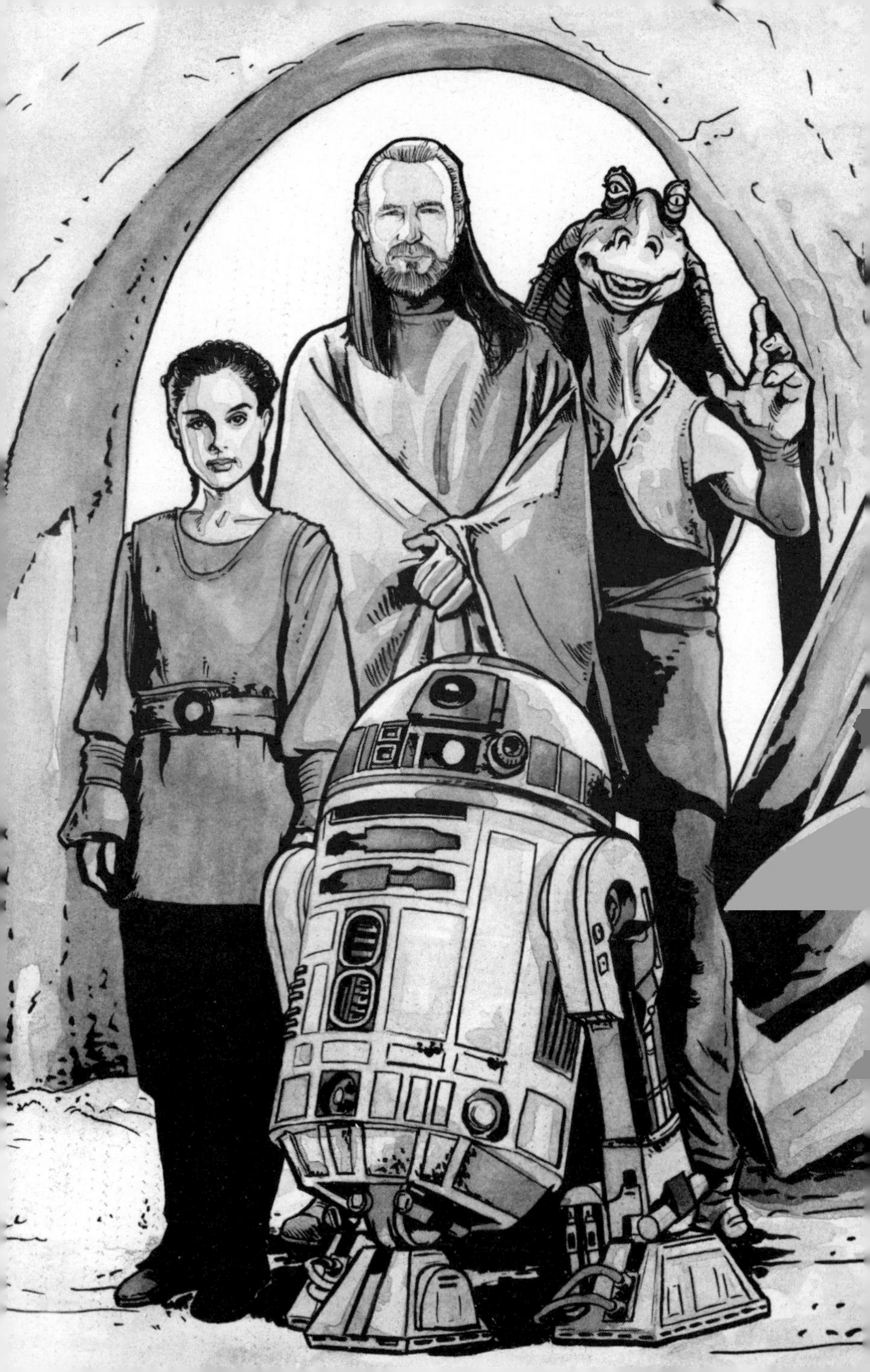

CHAPTER THREE

RACE FOR FREEDOM

When Anakin was nine years old, three outlanders walked into Watto's shop—and Anakin's life changed forever.

The leader was a bearded man in a poncho. His ship was damaged and needed a new hyperdrive generator. Watto took him and his astromech droid out back to look for the part. The other two strangers stayed in the shop with Anakin. One, a gangly humanoid with long ears, started looking around the shop and knocking stuff over. But Anakin was transfixed by the third off-worlder—a girl a few years older than he was. She was

so beautiful that Anakin asked if she was an angel—
he'd heard about angels from starship pilots refueling
at Mos Espa.

The girl wasn't an angel—and she angered Anakin
by looking shocked when she learned he was a slave.
But she seemed kind. When she and her friends left,
Watto fumed about arrogant outlanders, but Anakin was
curious about the visitors. He followed them. When a
sandstorm swept in, he led the group to his house to
take cover.

Anakin learned that the leader was named Qui-Gon Jinn, the humanoid was a Gungan named Jar Jar Binks, the astromech was R2-D2, and the girl was named Padmé. When Anakin spotted a lightsaber under Qui-Gon's cloak, he realized the man was a Jedi Knight.

That gave Anakin hope. Surely Qui-Gon was on Tatooine to free the slaves—after all, slavery was against Republic law, and the Jedi Knights were champions of peace and justice. But Qui-Gon, looking a bit sad, told Anakin that was not why he had come. Instead, he was on a secret mission to take Padmé to Coruscant, a planet in the galaxy's Core. Unfortunately, their ship had been damaged. Watto had the parts they needed for repairs, but he wouldn't accept Qui-Gon's Republic currency—and the Jedi had nothing to trade.

Anakin knew Watto's weakness was gambling, and came up with an idea. Anakin proposed that Qui-Gon tell Watto that he had a podracer of his own. Anakin told the Jedi that he could use the racer that Anakin had secretly built. Then he could offer to sponsor Anakin to compete in the next day's podrace, called the Boonta Eve Classic. If Anakin won, the prize money would be enough to pay for the parts, and Qui-Gon could repair his ship.

Qui-Gon agreed to Anakin's plan. The Jedi from distant Coruscant was intrigued by the slave boy from Tatooine.

Shmi trusted Qui-Gon and told him the secret of Anakin's birth. Qui-Gon then tested Anakin's blood to measure his level of midi-chlorians. Midi-chlorians were microscopic life-forms that existed in symbiosis with living things. They embodied the will of the Force, a mysterious energy field that bound the galaxy together. Anakin's midi-chlorian count was extraordinarily high, which meant he had enormous potential with the Force.

THE RACECOURSES WERE TREACHEROUS WITH TIGHT TWISTS AND TURNS THROUGH ROCKY CANYONS. ANAKIN'S ABILITY TO FLY A PODRACER MADE PEOPLE THINK HE HAD SUPERHUMAN REFLEXES, BUT THAT WASN'T TRUE. INSTEAD, WITHOUT KNOWING IT, ANAKIN USED THE FORCE TO SEE THINGS BEFORE THEY HAPPENED, ALLOWING HIM TO ANTICIPATE EVENTS AND TAKE ACTION.

Qui-Gon believed Anakin had been conceived by the midi-chlorians, and remembered an ancient Jedi prophecy that said a Chosen One would bring the light side and the dark side of the Force into balance. Qui-Gon believed Anakin was the Chosen One, and that their meeting was the will of the Force.

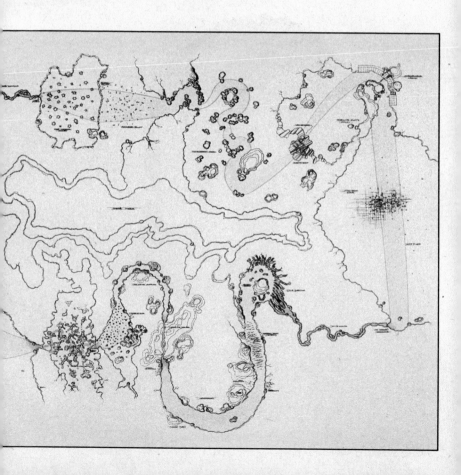

Qui-Gon negotiated a deal with Watto: the junk dealer would pay the entry fee for the race and let Anakin fly the pod that Qui-Gon claimed was his own. If Anakin won, Watto would get the winnings and give Qui-Gon the parts he needed. If Anakin lost, Qui-Gon would give the Toydarian his damaged ship.

PODRACING

Fast and dangerous, podracing is popular in the Outer Rim, with daring pilots flying customized speeders through rugged landscapes. Pilots need to be small and have fast reflexes, so few humans have ever succeeded at the sport. Intimidation is part of podracing, and most spectators don't mind if there is cheating, as long as it's done sneakily.

But Watto didn't bet on Anakin. He was certain Sebulba would win—after all, the Dug always did. So Qui-Gon cleverly offered him another bet: his pod (which actually was Anakin's, and therefore already belonged to Watto) against freedom for Anakin and Shmi. Watto refused, arguing that a pod was worth one slave but not

two. The Toydarian rolled a chance cube to determine whether the bet would be for Shmi or Anakin, and didn't notice when Qui-Gon quietly used the Force to ensure the cube indicated Anakin. If the boy won the race, Qui-Gon would be able to pay for the necessary parts for his ship, and Anakin would be freed from slavery.

Qui-Gon watched patiently beside an anxious Shmi as the podrace began. Anakin's pod stalled at the starting line, but he then rapidly caught up with the race's leaders, rocketing through the caves and canyons of Tatooine as the crowd roared. Sebulba was up to his old tricks and tried to sabotage Anakin's racer, but Anakin overcame it and then caught the Dug on the third and final lap of the race, where their pods became entangled. Sebulba's engine failed, and what was left of the Dug's pod crashed into the sand as Anakin raced across the finish line. Anakin had won!

Watto reluctantly honored his wager with Qui-Gon, but refused to let the Jedi buy Shmi's freedom as well. Anakin's joy turned to sorrow—he was free to go to Coruscant, but his mother would have to remain on Tatooine as a slave. Shmi wanted what was best for her son. She said, "You can't stop change any more than you can stop the suns from setting." Anakin promised his mother that he would come back and free her. Shmi urged him to be brave and not look back.

On the way to Qui-Gon's starship, the two were attacked by a tattooed warrior with a double-bladed lightsaber. Anakin rushed to the ship, where he met Qui-Gon's Padawan, Obi-Wan Kenobi. The ship took off and skimmed the sandy landscape with the gangplank lowered. As soon as Qui-Gon escaped the dark warrior, the crew raced into space, leaving Tatooine behind.

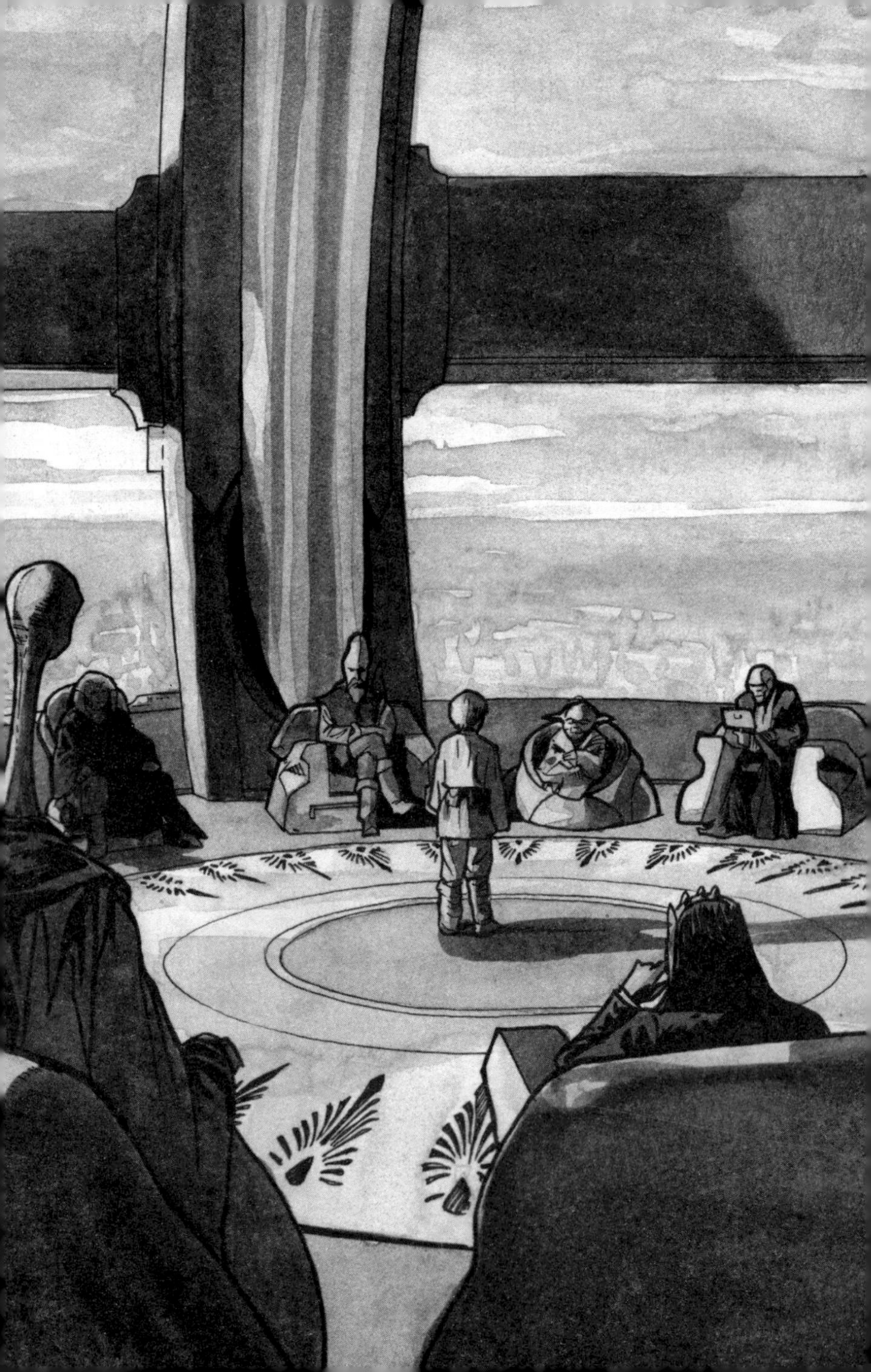

CHAPTER FOUR

THE NEW PADAWAN

Coruscant was like nothing Anakin had seen before—a planet whose entire surface was covered with massive skyscrapers. Qui-Gon brought Anakin before the Jedi Council there. Qui-Gon had told the Council that Anakin was a focal point of the Force and requested that they test his Force powers. The Jedi Masters—led by Yoda and Mace Windu—did so, then questioned the boy. They sensed that Anakin missed his mother and feared losing her.

Angry, Anakin asked what that had to do with anything, which led to a sharp reply from Yoda: "Fear leads to anger, anger leads to hate, hate leads to suffering."

The Council admitted that Anakin had great potential with the Force, but they refused to train him as a Jedi, telling Qui-Gon that he was too old. The Jedi identified Force-sensitive people as babies and raised them as part of the Jedi Order before they could form emotional attachments with their families. The Jedi thought such attachments were dangerous. Emotions could cloud a Jedi's mind and lead to fear and anger, which would leave a Jedi vulnerable to the dark side of the Force.

A frustrated Qui-Gon decided to defy the Council. He was certain it was the will of the Force that Anakin be trained as a Jedi. For him, that was more important than the Order's decision. He took Anakin with him to the planet Naboo. There, they learned that Padmé was actually Naboo's queen. She hoped to enlist Jar Jar's fellow Gungans to fight the Trade Federation that had invaded the usually peaceful planet.

During the Battle of Naboo, Qui-Gon told Anakin to

THE JEDI ORDER

The Jedi served as the Republic's peacekeepers for millennia, overseen by a council of Jedi Masters who met at the Order's principal temple on Coruscant. Babies who tested as powerful with the Force are considered to be "Force-sensitive." They are raised as younglings in Jedi temples, with the most capable becoming Padawans, then Jedi Knights, and finally Jedi Masters.

hide in the cockpit of a starfighter, but Anakin found himself flying that very starfighter into orbit. Showing off his amazing piloting skills, he destroyed the battleship that controlled the Trade Federation's battle droids, and returned to Naboo as a hero. But he learned that Qui-Gon had been killed, struck down in a lightsaber duel by the same warrior they had fled from on Tatooine.

Obi-Wan had then attacked the warrior, cutting him in two.

Dying, Qui-Gon begged Obi-Wan to train Anakin—a promise Obi-Wan vowed to keep. Yoda reluctantly agreed, but the Jedi Master warned Obi-Wan that he feared Anakin's training would lead to grave danger.

And so Anakin Skywalker became Obi-Wan Kenobi's Padawan over the objections of Jedi Masters Yoda and Mace Windu. Over the next decade, Anakin learned to open himself to the Force, proving himself as a pilot and lightsaber duelist. And he and Obi-Wan, once suspicious of each other, became as close as brothers.

But siblings fight—and Anakin and Obi-Wan often clashed as master and apprentice, with Anakin complaining that Obi-Wan was holding him back. Anakin also knew that important members of the Jedi Order hadn't wanted him to be trained in the first place. He wondered if the teachers who corrected him during training were trying to help, or put him in his place. His fellow Jedi apprentices knew about the rumors that

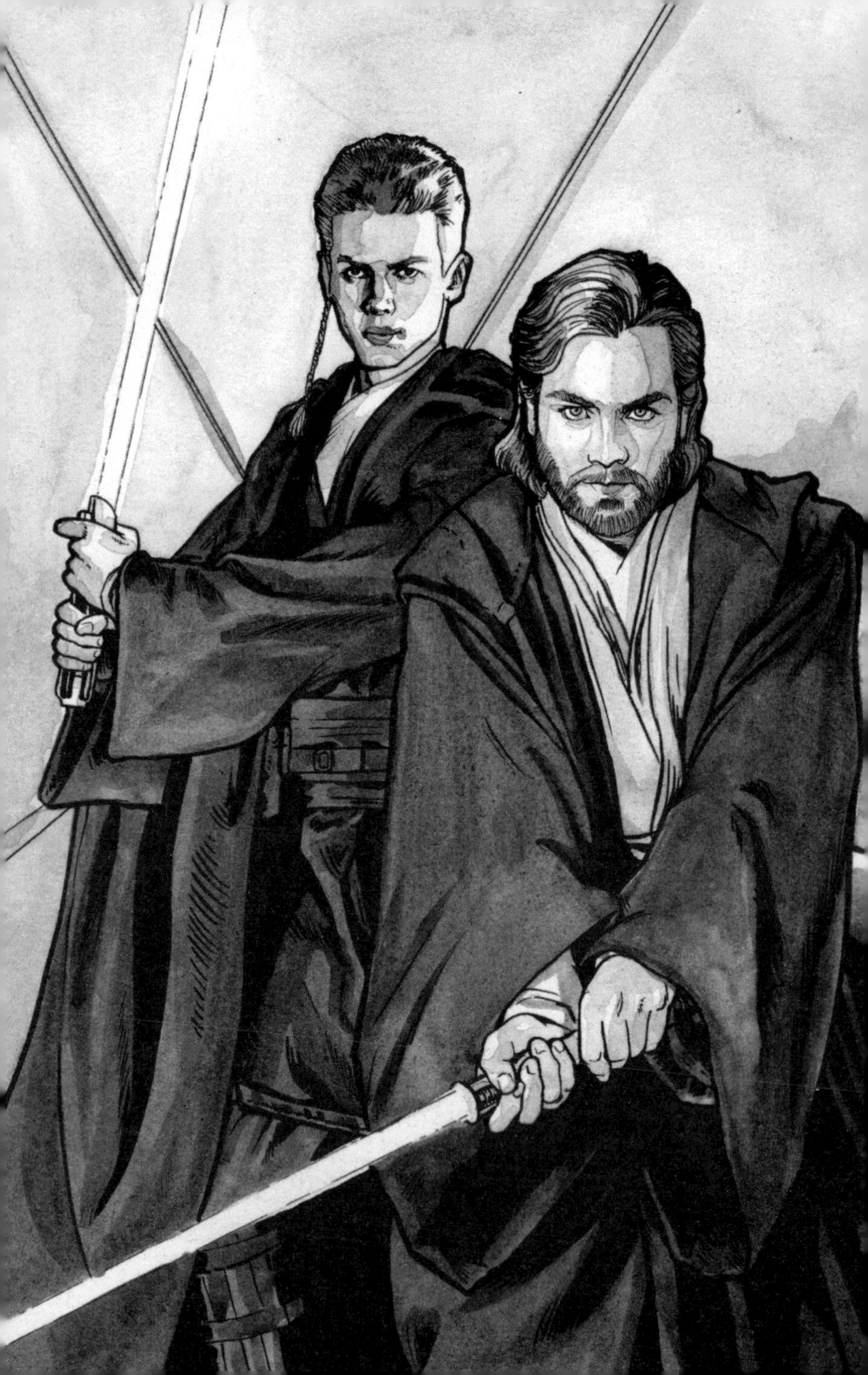

Anakin was the Chosen One of Jedi prophecy, and he found it hard to make friends. His training was often lonely, and he spent hours in his quarters tinkering with broken machinery he'd scavenged on trips out of the Jedi Temple.

Anakin also missed his mother and worried about her. The Jedi made no move to free Tatooine's slaves, and seemed indifferent to Anakin's fears about what had happened to Shmi. Obi-Wan tried to explain that the Jedi followed orders from the Republic's Senate, and couldn't fix every injustice in the galaxy. Also, he tried to remind Anakin of the danger of emotional attachments. But to Anakin, the issue seemed very clear: his mother was still a slave, and no one seemed interested in helping her or the other slaves. Sometimes Anakin felt that by avoiding emotional attachments, the Jedi had lost touch with the people they claimed to serve.

During his adventures with Obi-Wan, Anakin became even more powerful in the Force. But his emotions were stronger as well—and more conflicted than ever.

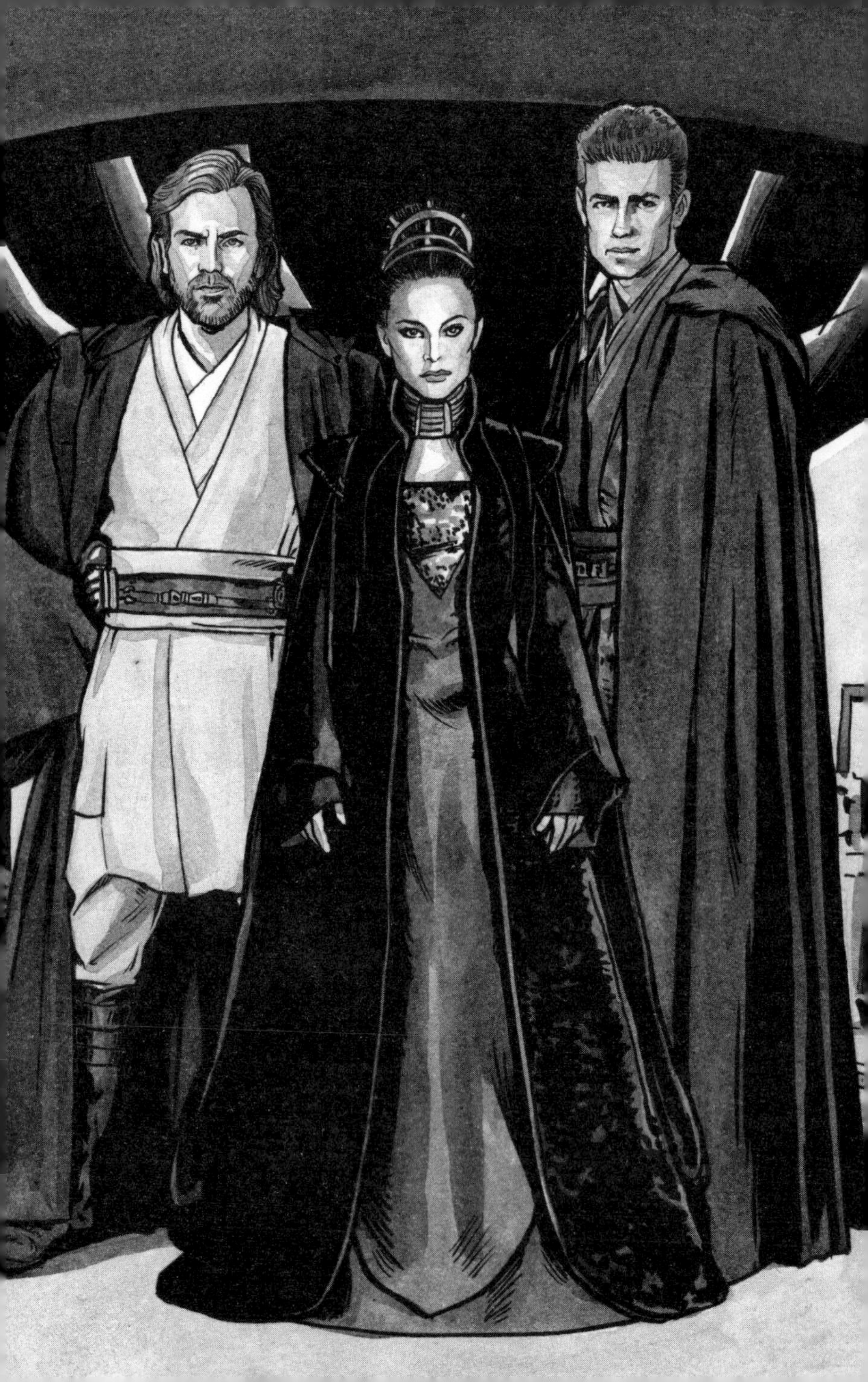

CHAPTER FIVE

RETURN TO TATOOINE

A decade after entering the Jedi Order, Anakin was reunited with Padmé Amidala. Padmé was now Naboo's senator. She had become a powerful voice in the Senate, and her strong opinions had put her in danger. The Republic's Supreme Chancellor was originally from Naboo as well. Supreme Chancellor Palpatine had taken a special interest in Anakin's Jedi career. When it became clear that Padmé needed protection, he assigned Obi-Wan and Anakin to protect the young senator from potential assassins.

Anakin found Padmé every bit as lovely as he had

when he first met her on Tatooine. His attraction to Padmé set his emotions boiling, even though he knew a Jedi should deny such feelings.

After Anakin and Obi-Wan foiled a second attempt to kill Padmé, Obi-Wan decided to investigate the assassin's background. Meanwhile, Anakin accompanied Padmé to Naboo as her bodyguard. The two hid in a beautiful villa in Naboo's Lake Country. In this peaceful place, Anakin surrendered to his feelings and kissed Padmé. After a moment, Padmé pulled away. She knew that as a senator and Jedi they had to think of their responsibilities, not romance. But that kiss had changed everything. Anakin couldn't stop thinking of Padmé, and she found herself falling in love with him, too.

But Anakin began having nightmares about his mother—dreams that she was in pain and danger. Anakin knew his dreams weren't like most people's— he had always been able to see things before they happened. He became increasingly frightened about what had happened to his mother on Tatooine—and felt more guilty about never having returned to free her, as he'd promised.

Finally he could stand it no longer. He told Padmé he had to go to Tatooine to help his mother. To his surprise, Padmé agreed to go with him. That way he could still protect her from harm, and not break his word to the Jedi.

There is no emotion, there is peace.
There is no ignorance, there is knowledge.
There is no passion, there is serenity.
There is no chaos, there is harmony.
There is no death, there is the Force.

THE JEDI CODE WAS A SET OF RULES FOR MEMBERS OF THE JEDI ORDER.

As soon as he arrived in Mos Espa, Anakin found Watto at his junk shop. His old master had fallen on hard times. Watto told Anakin that he no longer owned Shmi—he'd sold Anakin's mother to a moisture farmer named Cliegg Lars, who'd freed Shmi from slavery and married her.

At the Lars farm, Cliegg had grim news for Anakin and Padmé. Shmi had been kidnapped by a group of Tusken Raiders a month earlier. Cliegg and a search party had attempted to rescue her, but the Tuskens had driven them away.

Cliegg doubted Shmi was still alive, but Anakin wouldn't listen. He borrowed a fast vehicle called a swoop from Cliegg's son, Owen, and raced off into the desert in search of his mother.

A group of Jawas helped guide Anakin to a Tusken camp deep in the Jundland Wastes. He slipped inside and found Shmi. She was near death, having been badly hurt as part of the Tuskens' strange rituals. Shmi awoke long enough to realize Anakin was there, and managed to tell him how much she loved him and how proud of him she was. And then she died in his arms.

Anakin tried to control his emotions, but his rage and pain became a tidal wave of Force power. Igniting his lightsaber, he slaughtered the Tusken Raiders—not just the warriors, but the women and children in the

LIGHTSABER

The lightsaber is the weapon of a Jedi. It is built around a kyber crystal, and the brightly colored crystal generates the glowing blade. Jedi are formidable warriors, combining dueling skills with Force-heightened senses and reflexes, but they prefer to use their lightsabers in defense or as focal points for meditation. Younglings find crystals and construct their own sabers as part of their journey along the Jedi path.

camp, too. Then, numb with shock, Anakin brought his mother's body back to the Lars farm.

A tearful Anakin told Padmé what he'd done—and swore that he would become the most powerful Jedi ever, so powerful that he would be able to save the people he loved from dying. He hadn't been strong enough to save his mother, but he wouldn't fail again.

That vow would have terrible consequences—for Anakin and for the galaxy.

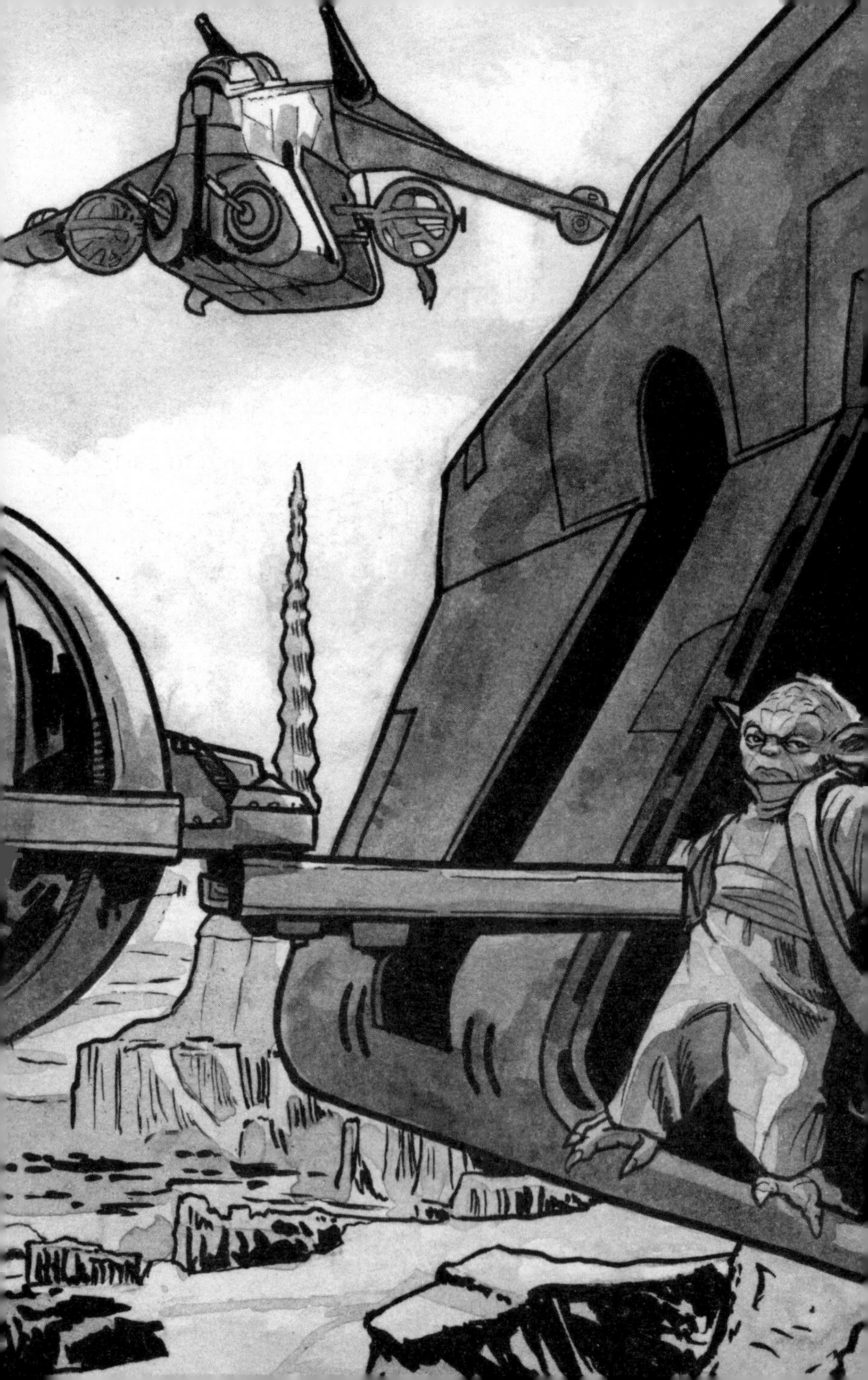

CHAPTER SIX

GENERAL IN THE CLONE WARS

Meanwhile, the galaxy was careening closer to war. All this time, Obi-Wan had been tracking Padmé's would-be assassin. The search led him to Geonosis, where he was taken prisoner by Count Dooku. Dooku was a former Jedi who was now the leader of the Separatist political movement. As soon as they heard, Anakin and Padmé rushed to save Obi-Wan, but they were captured and sentenced to death alongside Anakin's Jedi Master.

The Jedi launched a rescue mission, with Yoda leading an army of clones. The clones had been created for the Republic long before the current political crisis, and they were bioengineered for loyalty and obedience to their commanding officers.

This rescue mission on Geonosis became the first battle of the Clone Wars. Anakin and Obi-Wan tried to capture Dooku before he could escape. Enraged by Dooku's treachery and the fact that he had hired

assassins to take Padmé's life, Anakin unwisely attacked the former Jedi and lost the lower half of one arm in a lightsaber duel. Yoda's arrival was the only thing that prevented Anakin and Obi-Wan from being killed. Dooku managed to escape.

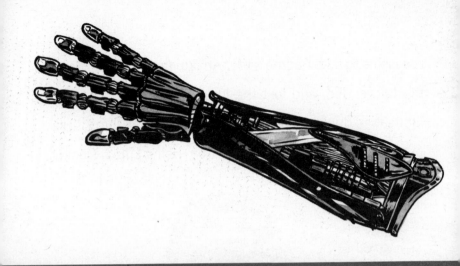

AFTER ANAKIN LOST PART OF HIS ARM FIGHTING COUNT DOOKU, HE RECEIVED A CYBERNETIC REPLACEMENT.

Anakin received a new mechanical arm, and later secretly married Padmé in a ceremony on Naboo.

The Clone Wars engulfed the galaxy, with the Republic's new clone armies fighting Dooku's battle droids on countless planets. The Jedi reluctantly agreed to put aside their traditional role as negotiators and peacekeepers and became generals, leading the clones and taking orders from Supreme Chancellor Palpatine.

Anakin became one of the heroes of the Clone Wars. He was promoted from Padawan to Jedi Knight

THE SITH

In ancient times the Sith were renegade Force users who focused
on anger and fear to gain power from the dark side of the Force.
The Jedi thought they'd destroyed the Sith a thousand years before
the Clone Wars, but the order had survived in secret by adopting a
new tradition: there were only two Sith at a time, a master and an
apprentice.

AHSOKA TANO

A young Togruta, Ahsoka Tano's Force-sensitivity was discovered in
infancy by Jedi Master Plo Koon, who brought her to Coruscant
for training. Yoda, the Jedi Order's Grand Master, later assigned the
headstrong Padawan to Anakin Skywalker during the Clone Wars.
After leaving the Jedi Order, Ahsoka reemerged as a key member of
the early Rebellion against the Empire.

and given charge of a legion of clone troopers led by the brave Captain Rex. Yoda knew Anakin had become crucial to the Republic war effort. Yet he was deeply worried about him. Yoda knew that Anakin commanded enormous Force powers, yet the young Jedi was often ruled by his emotions and his attachments to others.

Yoda decided to assign Anakin a Padawan, Ahsoka Tano. Anakin would have to teach Ahsoka to be patient and obey the Jedi Council—lessons he himself could use help learning. But more importantly, he and Ahsoka would have to go their separate ways once she was ready to become a Jedi Knight. Yoda hoped the experience of losing Ahsoka would teach Anakin the wisdom of letting go of his other, more dangerous, emotional attachments.

Anakin found Ahsoka a handful at first—she was impulsive and argumentative, much as he had been with Obi-Wan. Anakin never did teach her obedience to the Council, only how to disobey them more cleverly. But he did succeed in instructing her how to open herself to the Force and trust her feelings.

Anakin was often on the front lines of the war, fighting enemies such as Admiral Trench, Poggle the Lesser, Asajj Ventress, and Dooku. He grew ever closer to Palpatine, who became a mentor. Their relationship disturbed some high-ranking Jedi, who distrusted the Supreme Chancellor and resented his interference with Jedi business.

On a mission from the Jedi Council, Anakin, Obi-Wan, and Ahsoka answered a distress call and traveled to Mortis, a strange realm ruled by the Ones. There, Anakin had to make a difficult choice.

The Ones were three powerful, ancient beings with immense Force abilities. It was the Father's duty to keep his children—the light-side Daughter and dark-side Son—in balance. The Father had identified Anakin as the Chosen One. He pleaded with Anakin to remain in Mortis and take over his responsibilities when he died. The Father claimed that Anakin was the only one with the power to prevent the Son and Daughter from escaping and threatening the galaxy. He told Anakin that

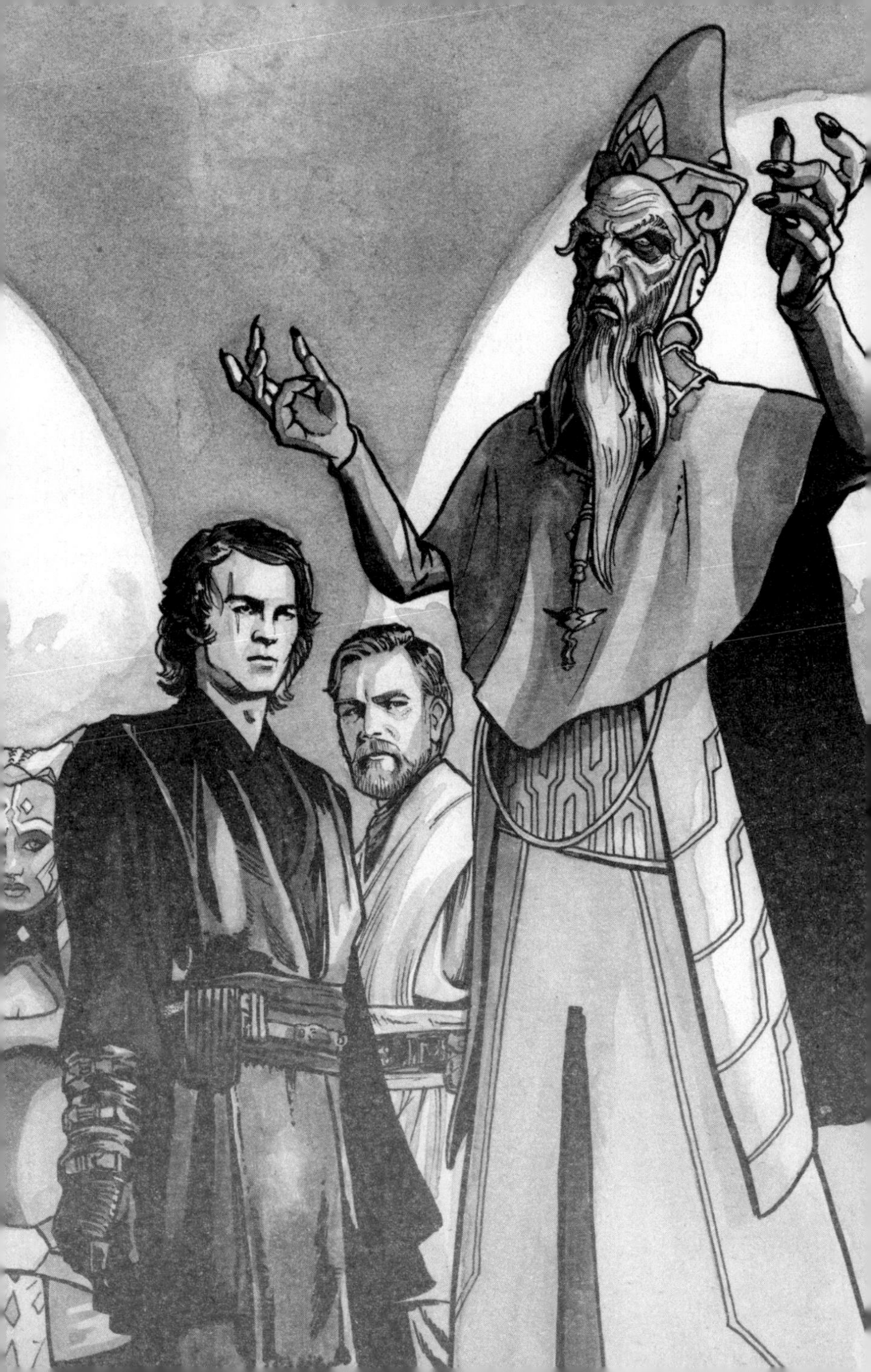

"too much dark or light would be the undoing of life as you know it." Anakin refused to stay on Mortis, and this strange encounter ended with all of the Ones destroyed.

The Father's last words to Anakin were a warning: "Beware of your heart."

Anakin and Ahsoka did form a tight bond, as Yoda had known they would. But the rest of Yoda's plan went disastrously wrong. Ahsoka was unfairly blamed

for attacks on the Jedi and expelled from the Order, then tried by a Republic military court. Knowing she was innocent, Anakin hunted desperately for evidence that would clear her name. He succeeded and Ahsoka was invited back, but she chose to walk away from the temple and seek her own path in the galaxy. Anakin felt that the Order had betrayed his Padawan, abandoning her in her time of need.

Anakin knew there were Jedi who still distrusted him despite all he'd done on the front lines of the Clone Wars. Now, their treatment of Ahsoka added to his own frustration with the Order.

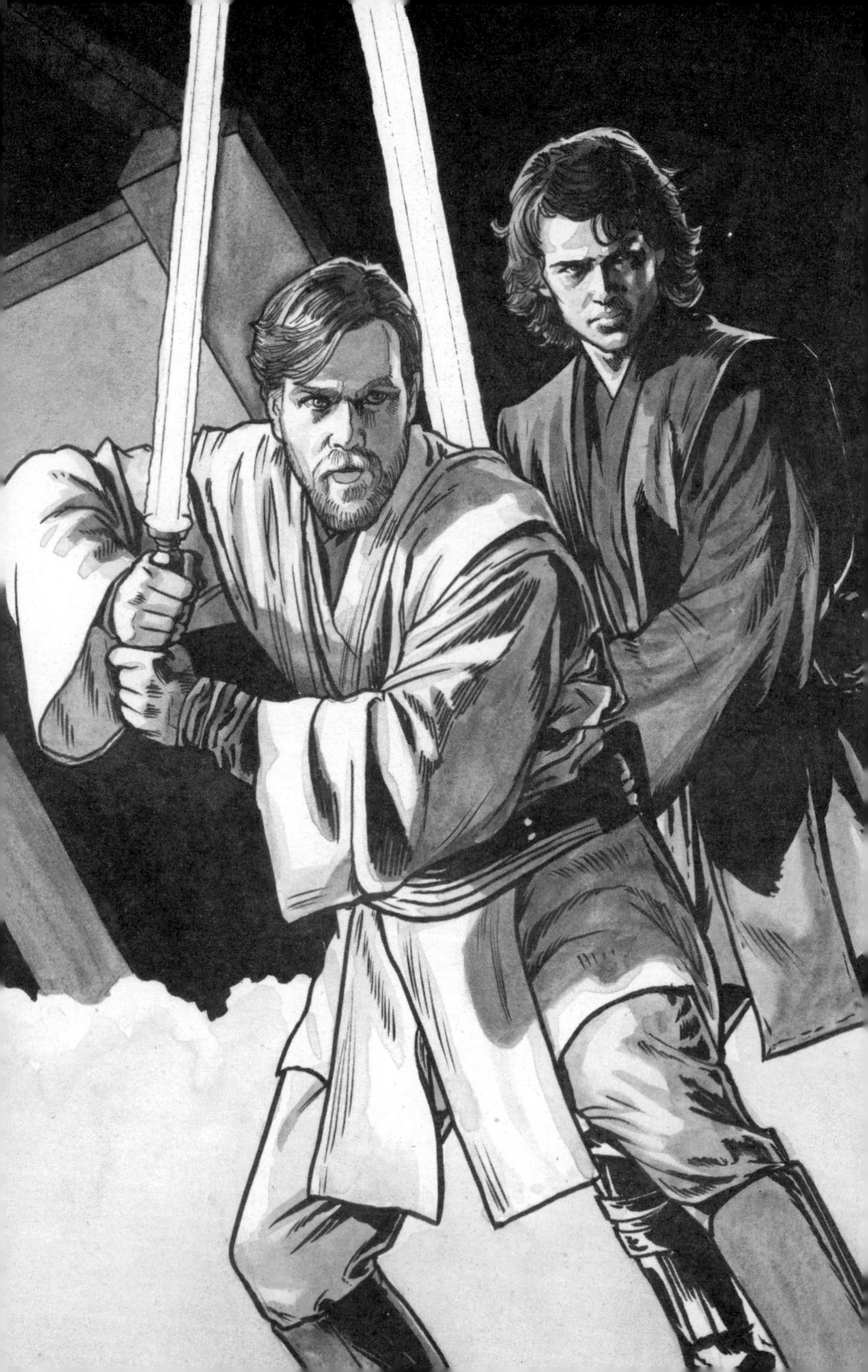

CHAPTER SEVEN

FALL OF THE REPUBLIC

During the Clone Wars, the Republic became a vast war machine, creating new battle fleets and clone armies and giving more and more emergency powers to Supreme Chancellor Palpatine. During this time, Anakin sometimes felt that the Jedi were limited in what they could accomplish. He once said to Obi-Wan, "If we aren't willing to do what it takes to win, we risk losing everything we try to protect." Obi-Wan saw it differently. His response was, "If we sacrifice our code, even for victory, we may lose that which is most important—our honor."

Gradually, the Republic's power overcame the Separatists, pushing them back into the Outer Rim. The Separatists launched what seemed like a desperate bid to avoid losing the war. General Grievous led a daring raid on Coruscant, kidnapping Palpatine and imprisoning the Supreme Chancellor on his flagship. Anakin and Obi-Wan raced to the rescue, infiltrating the ship and confronting Dooku in another three-way duel.

Dooku knocked Obi-Wan unconscious, but Anakin had grown far more powerful with the Force. He bested Dooku, slicing off the Separatist warlord's hands. The man who had caused the Republic so much pain was at Anakin's mercy. Goaded by Palpatine, Anakin killed Dooku with a flick of his lightsaber. He and Obi-Wan then returned to Coruscant having saved the Supreme Chancellor.

When they arrived, Anakin saw that Padmé was among the senators and dignitaries waiting for them. The war had frequently separated husband and wife, leaving each worried about the other. Now, Padmé had news for her husband: She was pregnant. That was another complication for them—Anakin would be expelled from the Jedi Order if their secret marriage was discovered—but Anakin was happy. The Clone Wars were winding down and they'd soon be parents of a child. They hoped their child would be born in Naboo's beautiful Lake Country, where they'd fallen in love.

But Anakin began having nightmares again—dreams in which Padmé died in childbirth. Anakin still blamed himself for failing to save his mother; he vowed he would not fail and lose Padmé.

Anakin faced other pressures, too. Palpatine appointed him to the Jedi Council as his personal representative. The Council reluctantly agreed, but they refused to grant him the title of Jedi Master. In addition, they asked him to spy on the Supreme Chancellor for

them. Anakin was angry about the Jedi's attempt to use him, but he had another reason to be angry. He believed that if he were a Jedi Master, he would have access to secret Jedi teachings that would make it possible for him to prevent Padmé's death.

Anakin's destiny took a fateful turn when Palpatine guessed what the Jedi had asked him to do. Palpatine warned Anakin that he thought the Jedi would try to overthrow him as Supreme Chancellor and take over the Republic. Palpatine also told him the story of Darth Plagueis, a Sith Lord who'd learned to use the Force to create life . . . and save people from death.

When Anakin asked if it was possible to learn that power, Palpatine's reply was simple: "Not from a Jedi."

Palpatine's suspicion of the Jedi was matched by the Jedi's suspicion of him. With Obi-Wan hunting down General Grievous, the Jedi waited to see if Palpatine would give up his emergency powers at the end of the war. They decided that if he did not, they would remove him from office and take temporary control of the Senate. To Anakin, that sounded a lot like what Palpatine had warned would happen. His own suspicion of the Jedi grew.

When Anakin told Palpatine that Obi-Wan had located Grievous, the Supreme Chancellor revealed an astonishing secret—he was really the Sith Lord Darth Sidious. Sidious had been the secret leader of both sides during the Clone Wars, and now he told Anakin that he could teach him the ways of the dark side— including how to save Padmé.

DARTH SIDIOUS

The secret Sith Lord, Darth Sidious, launched an audacious plan to gain control of the Republic, destroy the Jedi Order, and create a new, Sith-ruled empire. The galaxy knew Sidious as Sheev Palpatine, the senator from Naboo who'd been elected Supreme Chancellor a decade before the Clone Wars. Later, he ruled the galaxy as Emperor.

Deeply troubled by this information, Anakin returned to the Jedi Temple and told Mace Windu what he had learned. Windu and three other Jedi went on a mission to arrest Palpatine—but Mace ordered Anakin to stay behind. Anakin briefly obeyed, but then rushed to Palpatine's office, where he found Windu had Sidious cornered. Anakin told Windu that the Sith Lord must stand trial, but Mace replied that he was too dangerous, and raised his saber for the killing stroke. Anakin feared that he couldn't save Padmé without Sidious's teachings, and so ignited his own saber and cut off Windu's hand. Sidious then blasted the Jedi Master with Force lightning, sending him falling to his death.

Anakin had made his choice. He would do whatever Sidious asked in exchange for help saving Padmé. He became Sidious's apprentice, taking the name Darth Vader.

Sidious told Vader that he had to become much stronger with the dark side to save Padmé. He added that the Jedi had betrayed the Republic and were now

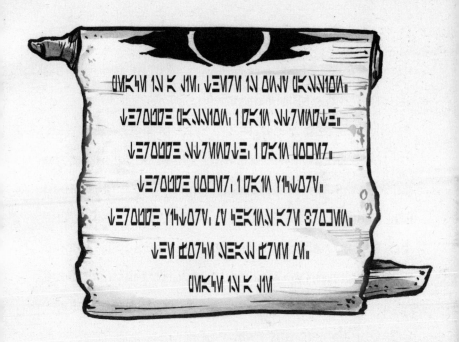

THE SITH CODE WAS AN INVERSION OF THE JEDI'S VALUES.

its enemies. Grimly determined, Darth Vader marched to the Jedi Temple with a garrison of clone troopers and killed the Jedi he had once fought alongside—even Padawans and younglings.

Meanwhile, Sidious contacted the clone commanders and ordered the soldiers to attack their generals. The clones had been bred for instinctive loyalty, and secret programming in their brains made it difficult for them to resist obeying commands. Within minutes, the Jedi Order was all but destroyed.

Sidious sent Vader to the lava planet Mustafar to kill the Separatist leaders, after which he promised the galaxy would be at peace. Obi-Wan—who had escaped execution by his own troops—returned to Coruscant and met Padmé, telling her what Anakin had done. Padmé didn't believe Obi-Wan and wouldn't tell him where Anakin had gone, but she then headed for Mustafar— with Obi-Wan stowing away on her ship.

On Mustafar, Padmé pleaded with her husband to come with her and leave everything behind. But Vader replied that they didn't have to do that. With his new powers he could save her and overthrow Sidious, allowing husband and wife to rule the galaxy. Padmé was horrified—and astonished when Obi-Wan appeared at the top of her ship's ramp.

When Vader saw his former master, he mistakenly concluded that Padmé had betrayed him. Overcome by rage, he choked her with the Force, leaving her

MUSTAFAR

A lava planet in the Outer Rim, Mustafar was the site of Darth Vader's duel with Obi-Wan Kenobi, and later became Vader's retreat. The Empire took Jedi to the fiery planet for interrogation, and Vader later returned there to meditate and amplify his dark side powers.

unconscious. Obi-Wan intervened, and he and Vader began to duel. Obi-Wan defeated Vader, striking off his limbs and leaving him burning on the shores of a lava river. Obi-Wan thought Anakin had only minutes to live, and found himself unable to kill his former friend. Heartbroken, he took Anakin's lightsaber and fled.

Obi-Wan brought Padmé to Polis Massa, where she died after giving birth to twins—Luke and Leia. The children were split up, with Obi-Wan taking Luke to live with the Lars family on Tatooine while Leia was raised on Alderaan by Bail Organa and his wife. Padmé's funeral

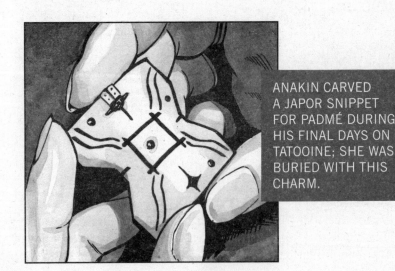

ANAKIN CARVED A JAPOR SNIPPET FOR PADMÉ DURING HIS FINAL DAYS ON TATOOINE; SHE WAS BURIED WITH THIS CHARM.

took place on Naboo, where she was laid to rest, still apparently pregnant to the rest of the galaxy.

Obi-Wan assumed Anakin had died, but he was wrong. Sidious had saved him, and took him to a medical center on Coruscant. Mechanical limbs replaced his arms and legs, while armor shielded his ruined body and machinery breathed for him. His face was sealed behind a black mask and helmet—the new face of Darth Vader.

Reborn as half-man, half-machine, Vader asked Sidious if Padmé was all right—only to have his Sith master reply that Vader had killed her in his anger. Anakin's actions had led to the very fate he'd tried to prevent—and he had been consumed by evil in the process.

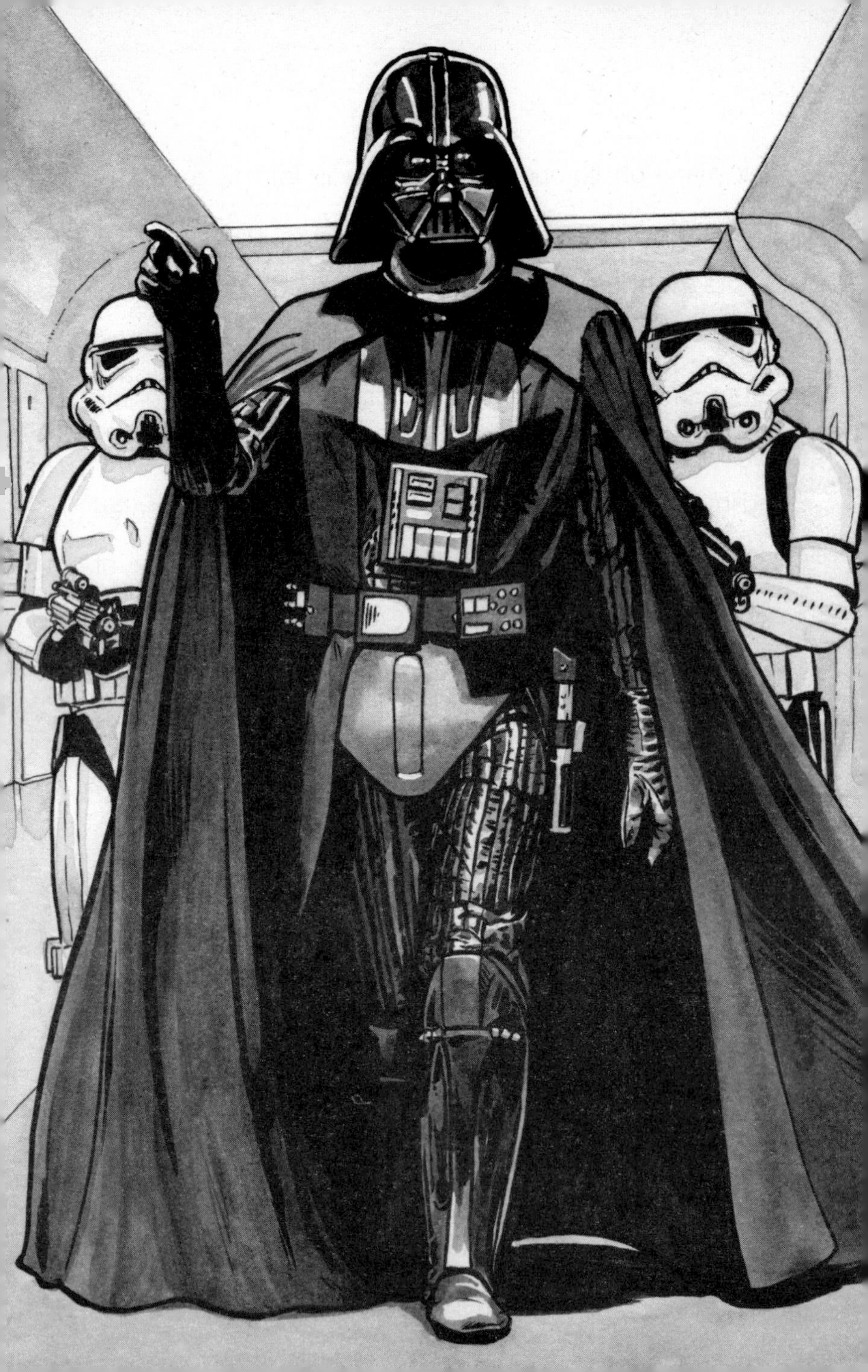

CHAPTER EIGHT

SERVANT OF THE EMPIRE

With the Separatists defeated and the Jedi destroyed, Palpatine declared an end to the Republic. He named himself Emperor of the First Galactic Empire—a supreme leader. While some citizens feared the unlimited power of the Emperor, many others thought the Empire's military would bring peace and stability.

Stormtroopers replaced clones in the Imperial military, which defeated outlaws and slavers, as well as arrested those who objected to Imperial rule. The Empire expanded rapidly into the Outer Rim, looking for new planets that had resources—minerals, crystals, crops, and workers—it could exploit.

Enemies of the Empire soon learned Palpatine had a terrifying new enforcer—the black-armored warrior known as Darth Vader.

Very few people knew Vader had once been Anakin Skywalker, the Jedi hero—just as very few knew Emperor Palpatine was a Sith Lord. But all feared Darth Vader. He hunted down fugitive Jedi, killing them or taking them to Imperial prisons. This mission culminated with a confrontation with his former Padawan, Ahsoka Tano. Ahsoka had joined a band of rebels set on defeating the Empire. As a traitor of the Empire, she and her friends were prime targets for Vader and his red-bladed lightsaber. He made it his duty to personally execute traitors.

Despite now ruling the galaxy, Sidious continued to follow Sith traditions. The Sith had escaped the Jedi's notice for centuries by limiting their ranks to just two: a master and an apprentice. But unlike the Jedi, this was not a relationship based on trust. Master and

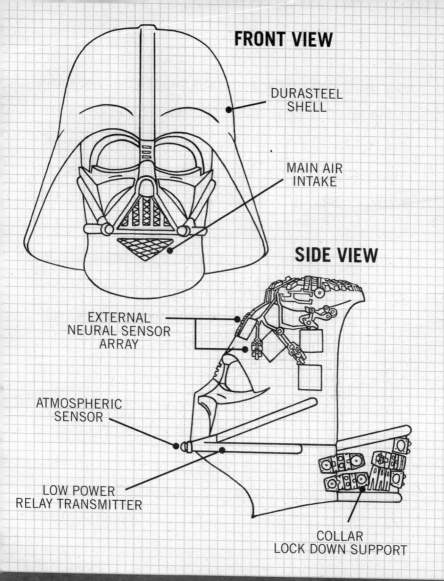

FRONT VIEW

DURASTEEL SHELL

MAIN AIR INTAKE

SIDE VIEW

EXTERNAL NEURAL SENSOR ARRAY

ATMOSPHERIC SENSOR

LOW POWER RELAY TRANSMITTER

COLLAR LOCK DOWN SUPPORT

DARTH VADER'S BLACK ARMOR IS BOTH A PRISON AND A REFUGE. HE CANNOT LIVE WITHOUT IT. THE ARMOR CONCEALS HIS ROBOTIC LIMBS AND THE SYNTHETIC ORGANS THAT KEEP HIS DAMAGED BODY ALIVE. VADER'S NIGHTMARISH MASK BECOMES THE FACE HE DISPLAYS TO THE GALAXY AS THE EMPEROR'S ENFORCER.

apprentice constantly searched for any sign of weakness in the other. A weak master deserved to be destroyed and replaced by his or her apprentice, just as a weak apprentice deserved to lose his or her position to a more worthy student. In this way, the Sith remained as strong as possible.

Sidious constantly tested Vader, encouraging him to become more powerful with the dark side of the Force. Sidious wanted him to eliminate any remnant of Anakin Skywalker. Vader drew power from his anger and pain—raging at the loss of his wife and unborn child, at his betrayal by the Jedi, and at Obi-Wan for his near-fatal injuries.

The Emperor ordered Vader to assist the ruthless Grand Moff Tarkin, who was in charge of building the Death Star. The Death Star was a space station the size of a moon with a superlaser powerful enough to destroy a planet. As Anakin, Vader had served alongside Tarkin during the Clone Wars—now, Vader assisted Tarkin in battling anyone who opposed the Empire in the galaxy's

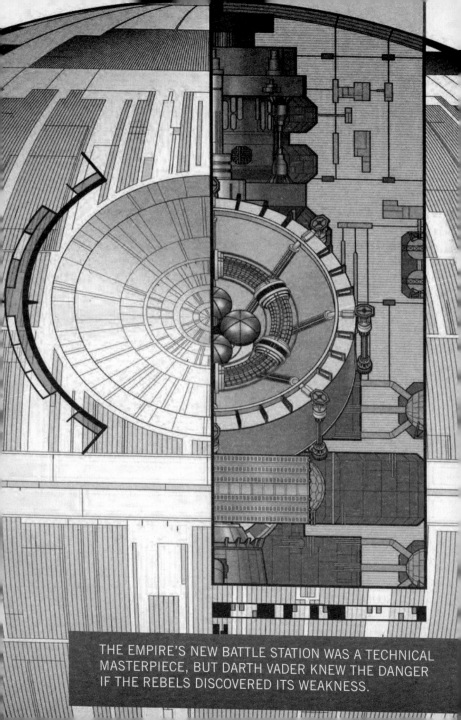

THE EMPIRE'S NEW BATTLE STATION WAS A TECHNICAL MASTERPIECE, BUT DARTH VADER KNEW THE DANGER IF THE REBELS DISCOVERED ITS WEAKNESS.

Outer Rim. But neither man was able to prevent the scattered resistance movements from uniting to create the Rebel Alliance. Sidious believed that once the Death Star was operational, no one in the galaxy would dare defy him. The Sith would rule forever.

The battle station was built in absolute secrecy. Scientists in the Empire's weapons programs spent decades developing it. As it neared completion, rebels learned of the Death Star's existence. They stole the Death Star plans and transmitted them to Leia Organa, Alderaan's princess and senator.

Vader, however, was in hot pursuit. His Star Destroyer captured Leia's ship over Tatooine. Vader didn't find the stolen plans, but he did find Leia, whom he accused of being part of the Rebel Alliance and a traitor. He ordered her taken to the Death Star as a prisoner. Learning that an escape pod had been jettisoned from the ship, he sent stormtroopers to Tatooine to find the plans.

Vader brutally questioned Leia, attempting to learn the location of the rebel base, but she resisted him.

Tarkin had another idea, and ordered the Death Star to set course for Alderaan, which he threatened to destroy. Leia told him that the rebels were on Dantooine— which was a lie—but Tarkin blew up her home planet of

Alderaan anyway, just to demonstrate the Death Star's horrific power.

But Vader would soon be forced to confront his own past. Leia had hidden the plans in the memory banks of R2-D2 and ordered the droid to take them to Obi-Wan Kenobi, who was in exile on Tatooine. R2-D2, with C-3PO in tow, did just that. Obi-Wan then arranged to travel to Alderaan so he could deliver the plans to the rebels, hiring the pilot of a beat-up freighter called the *Millennium Falcon*. But the Death Star captured the *Falcon* as soon as it approached the blasted remnants of Alderaan.

Obi-Wan and the others on the ship—a Wookiee, two humans, and two droids—needed to escape the Death Star. Obi-Wan decided to shut down the station's tractor beam so the *Falcon* could take off. Sneaking through the Death Star, Obi-Wan avoided being captured by stormtroopers, but Vader sensed his presence. Meanwhile, the *Falcon*'s other passengers rescued Leia from her cell.

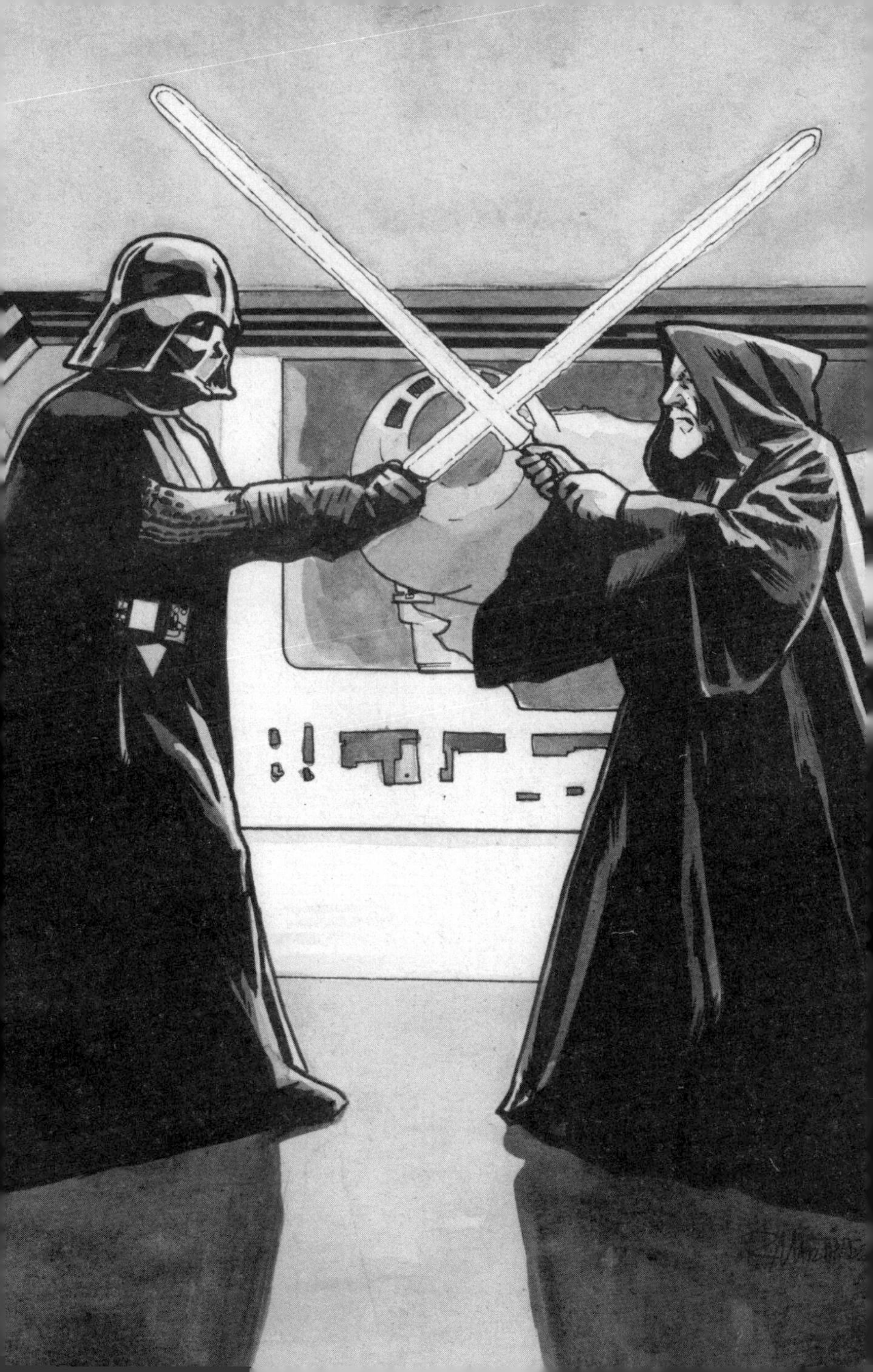

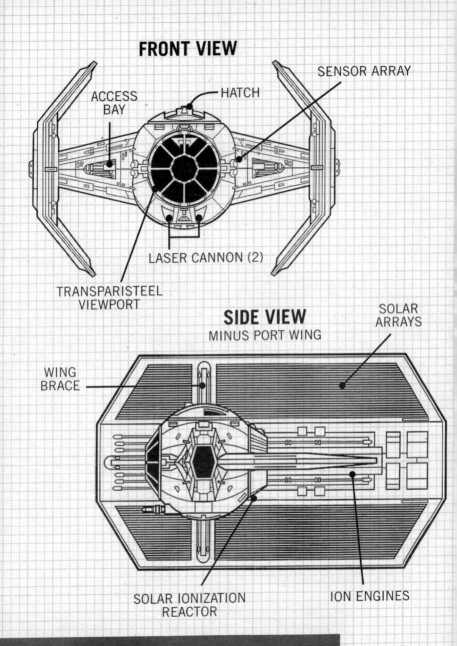

FRONT VIEW

SENSOR ARRAY

ACCESS BAY

HATCH

LASER CANNON (2)

TRANSPARISTEEL VIEWPORT

SIDE VIEW
MINUS PORT WING

SOLAR ARRAYS

WING BRACE

SOLAR IONIZATION REACTOR

ION ENGINES

DARTH VADER FLEW A TIE ADVANCED X1, A PROTOTYPE. UNLIKE STANDARD TIES, VADER'S FIGHTER HAD SHIELDS AND A HYPERDRIVE.

Vader tracked down Obi-Wan and confronted him before he could flee. The two once again dueled with their lightsabers. Obi-Wan warned Vader if that he struck his former master down, Obi-Wan would become more powerful than Vader could possibly imagine. Vader swung his lightsaber at Obi-Wan . . . and to his astonishment, the old Jedi simply vanished, leaving behind his robes and lightsaber.

While they battled, Princess Leia and her rescuers managed to board the *Millennium Falcon*. Then the *Falcon* raced away from the Death Star and escaped into hyperspace.

Vader wasn't worried; he'd ordered a homing beacon installed on the *Falcon*, and the Death Star followed the freighter to the Yavin system, site of the rebel base. The Death Star was moments away from being ready to fire. When it was in range, the battle station could destroy the rebel base with one laser blast, winning a huge victory for Darth Vader and the Empire.

Rebel starfighters attacked the station, with Vader

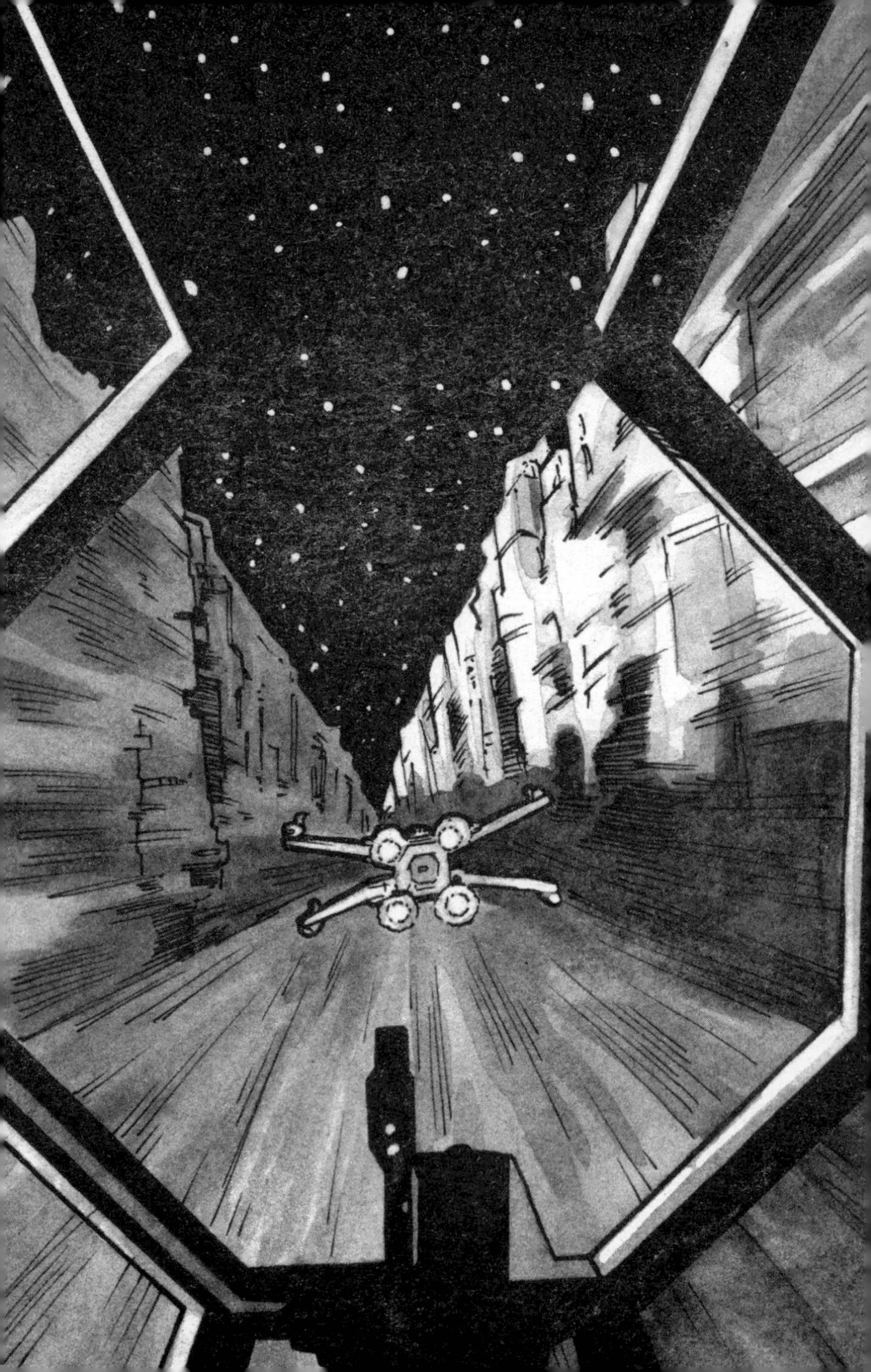

shooting many of them down in his customized TIE fighter. Vader sensed one of the last remaining rebel pilots was strong with the Force, but that would hardly be enough against a Dark Lord of the Sith. Vader prepared to fire—and looked up in disbelief as the *Millennium Falcon* charged at the Death Star, ruining Vader's attack. A moment later, the TIE fighter next to Vader's crashed into his own craft, sending the Sith Lord spinning helplessly off into deep space. That left the rebel pilot with a clear shot at the Death Star's one vulnerable spot, a small thermal exhaust port. The pilot fired, and moments later the battle station exploded into a cloud of glittering fragments. The rebels had won an enormous battle against the Empire.

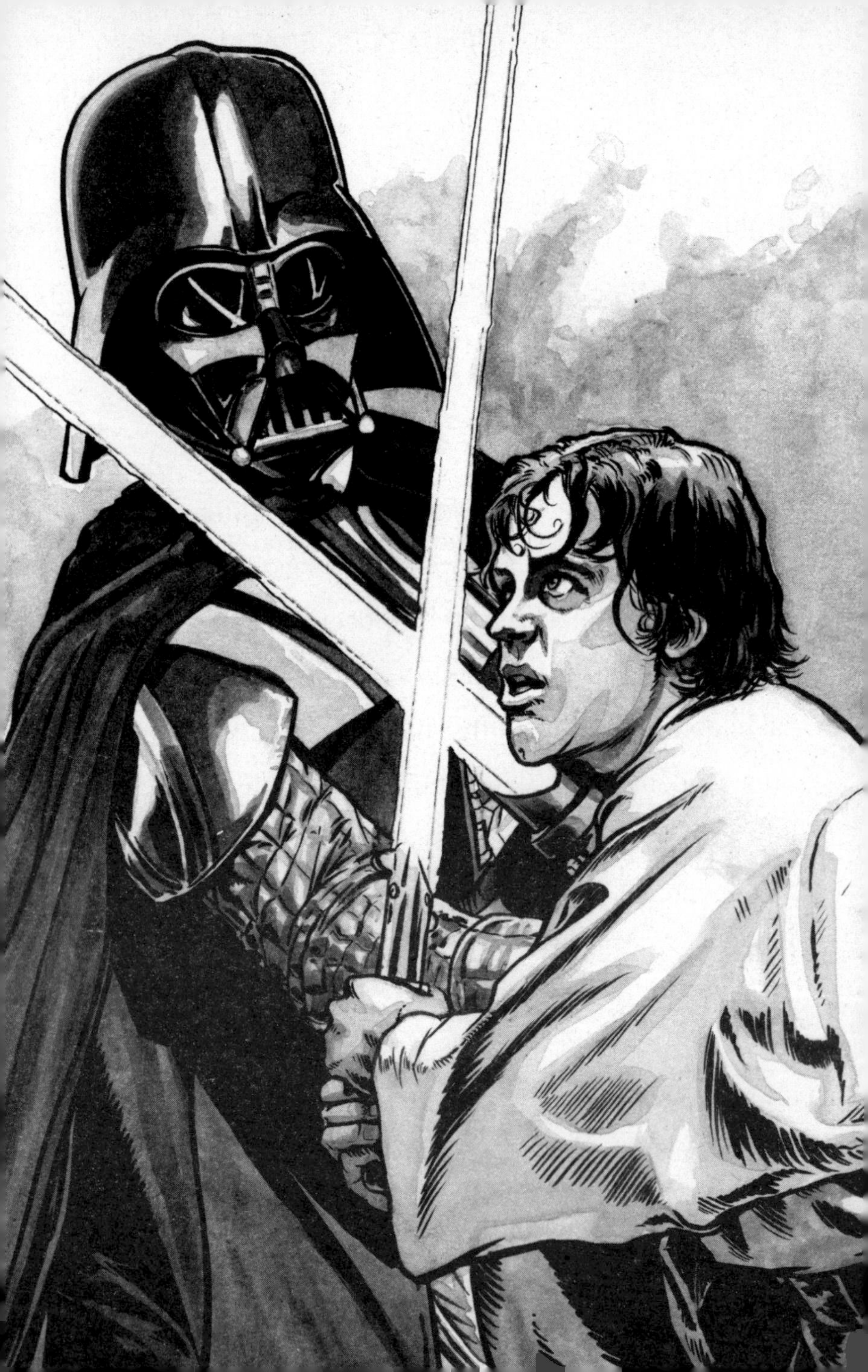

CHAPTER NINE

DARK LORD'S DISCOVERY

Vader returned to Palpatine's side. He was determined to punish the rebels and find the pilot who had destroyed the Death Star. He sensed the pilot's presence on Cymoon 1, where he confronted a young man who said that Vader had killed his father and Obi-Wan Kenobi. That young man was carrying Anakin's lightsaber.

Vader disarmed his opponent easily—he was little more than an untrained boy. But before Vader could strike him down, his rebel friends rescued him in an Imperial walker they'd captured. The rebels escaped

Cymoon 1, leaving Vader to conclude that Obi-Wan had trained an apprentice and given him Anakin's old lightsaber. Vader decided to find the boy—Obi-Wan's last hope—and turn him to the dark side of the Force.

Angry with Vader for his failure to defend the Death Star and capture the Cymoon rebels, Palpatine ordered his apprentice to serve Grand General Tagge—and dispatched Vader to Tatooine for negotiations with Jabba the Hutt, the underworld kingpin who ruled from a fortress in the planet's Dune Sea.

Vader saw both orders as an insult, but he realized that returning to Tatooine would allow him to seek the truth about the boy. Vader also wanted to investigate how Obi-Wan had spent his years in exile. After speaking with Jabba, he secretly arranged to hire a bounty hunter to find out about the boy and bring him back alive. The hunter—the infamous Boba Fett—failed to capture the boy, but discovered his name.

That name was Luke Skywalker.

Now Vader understood. The child he had thought

died with Padmé had lived, and had been raised in secrecy on Tatooine, with Obi-Wan watching over him. Vader began to plot how he could overthrow Darth Sidious. He would capture Luke and train him as his own apprentice, until father and son were strong enough to destroy the Emperor and rule the galaxy in his place.

THIS POSTER PROMOTED THE IMPERIAL NAVY'S SLEEK, NEW STAR DESTROYERS, DESIGNED TO HUNT DOWN REBEL FORCES. DARTH VADER'S SHIP WAS NAMED THE *EXECUTOR*.

When an Imperial probe droid discovered the rebels on the frozen planet Hoth, Vader led the attack from his flagship, the massive Super Star Destroyer *Executor*.

Luke eluded him, however, and the Emperor contacted Vader to test him yet again. Sidious told Vader that the young rebel who'd destroyed the Death Star was the offspring of Anakin Skywalker. Vader pretended he hadn't known about his son, appearing to still be loyal to his master. He then suggested that if Luke could be turned to the dark side, he might be a powerful ally for the Sith. When the idea intrigued the Emperor, Vader promised that Luke would join them or die.

The meeting left Vader more determined than ever to carry out his plan. Luke was now a pawn in the ongoing game between Vader and Sidious. Yes, Luke was untrained—but he was also powerful with the Force. And Vader knew that if he didn't turn Luke to the dark side of the Force and claim him as a Sith apprentice, his master would.

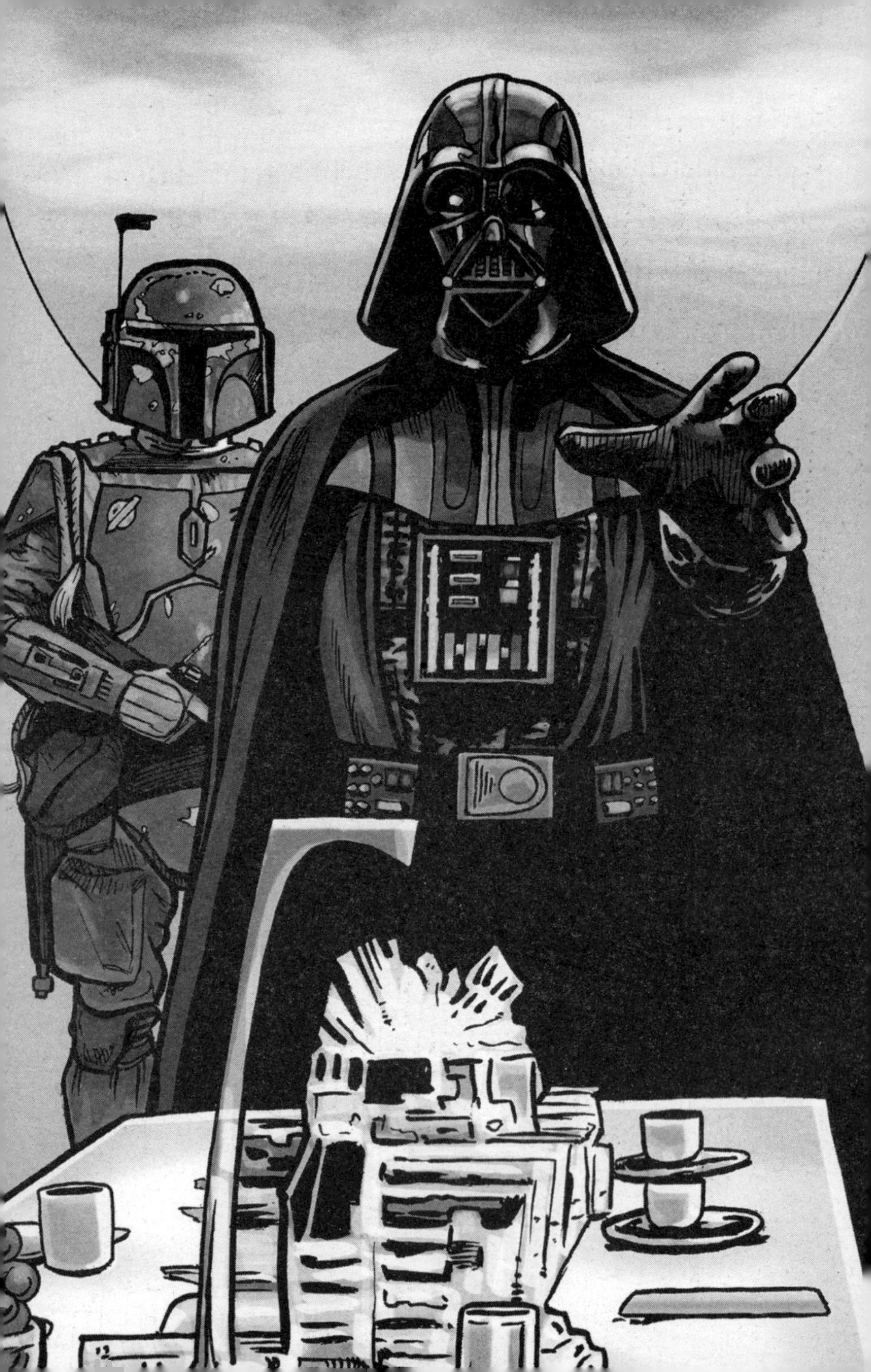

CHAPTER TEN

DUEL ON CLOUD CITY

The *Millennium Falcon* fled Hoth, but was unable to go into hyperspace and sought refuge in an asteroid field. Vader assumed Luke would be on the ship with its pilot, the smuggler Han Solo. Vader sent Imperial warships to scour the asteroids in search of the ship and summoned a quintet of bounty hunters—including Boba Fett—to join the hunt.

The *Falcon* escaped the Imperial dragnet, but Fett figured out that the ship was using its backup hyperdrive to limp to the Bespin system—where Han Solo's old smuggling comrade Lando Calrissian was

BOBA FETT

The Republic's clone troopers were behaviorally altered genetic copies of the bounty hunter Jango Fett, who raised an unaltered clone as his son, Boba. The galaxy's criminals came to fear the sight of Boba Fett's battered Mandalorian armor and the sound of his clanking spurs. Vader hired Fett for jobs he preferred not to trust to Imperial agents.

the administrator of the Cloud City mining colony. Fett alerted Vader, and the Dark Lord arrived before the rebels did.

Vader offered Calrissian a deal that was not really a deal at all: the Empire would ignore Cloud City's existence if Calrissian helped trap Solo and his friends, whom Vader would use as bait to attract his real target—Luke. Calrissian knew he couldn't fight the Imperial military and reluctantly agreed. He invited Han Solo, Princess Leia, and Han's copilot Chewbacca to a luncheon, where Vader and Fett were waiting.

Vader needed a way to imprison Luke for transport to a location where he could be turned to the dark side. The Dark Lord decided to entomb Luke in carbonite, but needed to make sure Luke would survive the freezing process. So he decided to test it on Solo before giving the smuggler with a price on his head to Boba Fett as a valuable bounty.

Solo survived and Vader ordered Calrissian to take Leia and Chewbacca to the *Executor* to face justice for

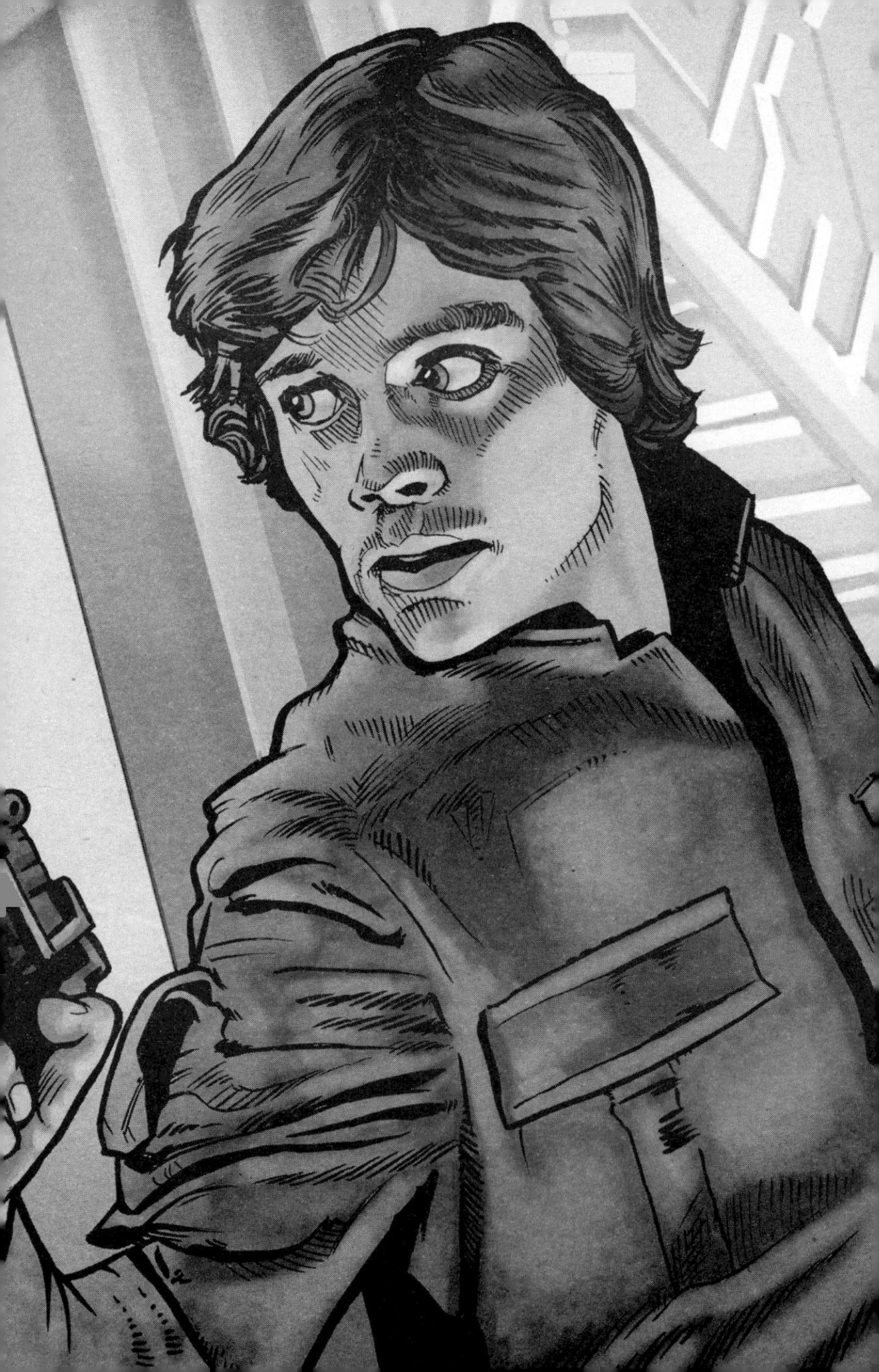

their crimes against the Empire. Then, having been informed that Luke had arrived on Cloud City, he waited for his son in the carbon-freezing chamber.

Luke had grown considerably in power and confidence since their last meeting—but young Skywalker was not a Jedi yet. He showed impressive ability in escaping Vader's trap, but his skills were no match for the power of the dark side. Vader broke down Luke's defenses, driving him along a narrow catwalk over a drop into a deep reactor shaft. In the midst of battle, he cut off the boy's hand.

While Luke clung with one hand to a metal sensor over the shaft, Vader told Luke that Obi-Wan had lied—that he, Darth Vader, was Luke's father. He asked Luke to join him, promising to complete his training, and told Luke that it was his destiny to destroy the Emperor. By combining their strengths, they could rule the galaxy as father and son.

But then Luke did something completely unexpected—he simply let go of the atmosphere sensor,

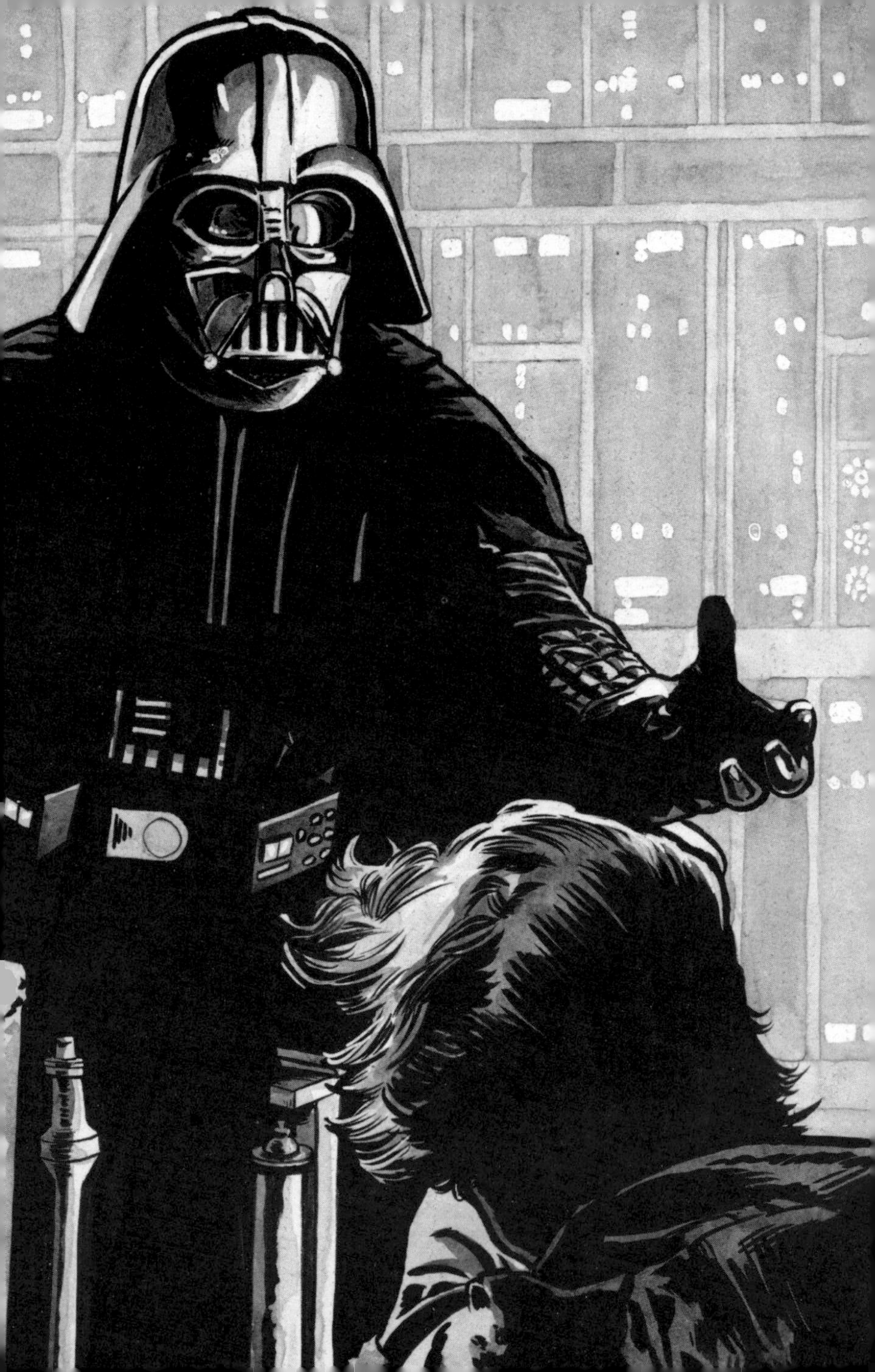

allowing himself to plunge down the reactor shaft. Vader summoned his stormtroopers and learned that Calrissian had betrayed him and escaped with Leia and Chewbacca aboard the *Falcon*. The fleeing rebels then doubled back to save Luke, who'd survived his plunge into the depths of Cloud City, and escaped.

Vader had found his lost son and told him of his destiny—but Luke had rejected the chance to join his father, ruining Vader's plans.

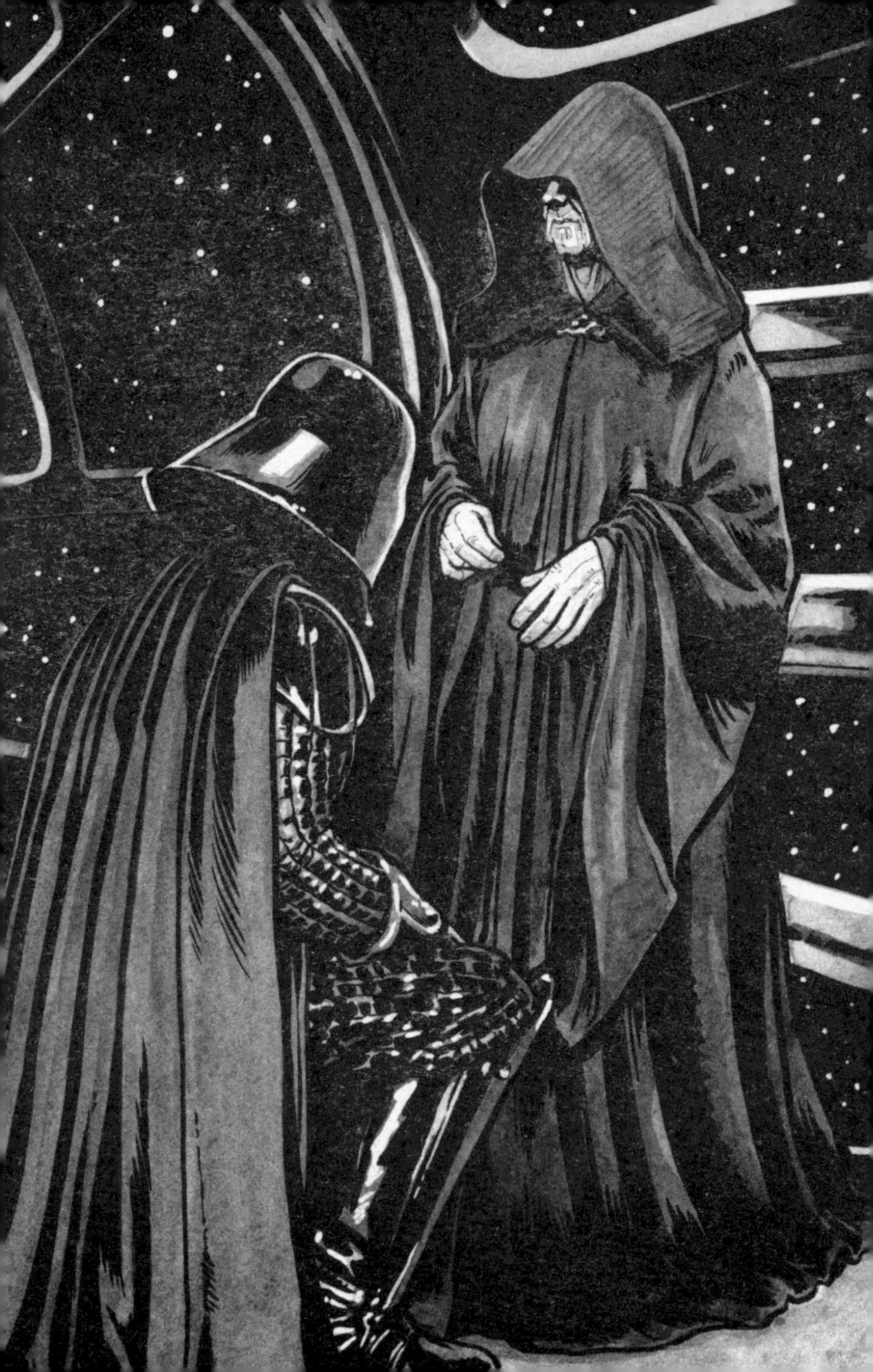

CHAPTER ELEVEN

ENDGAME AT ENDOR

Dismayed and disturbed by the events on Cloud City, Vader returned to his master. Vader had failed, and he no longer saw a way to use Luke to overthrow Sidious. If Darth Sidious learned of Vader's treachery, he would undoubtedly kill his apprentice.

The Emperor sent Vader to the second Death Star, now nearing completion at Endor. Sensing Vader's feelings, he told his apprentice that in time, Luke would seek him out. The Emperor said the boy had grown in power, and it would take both their efforts to turn him to the dark side. But he assured his apprentice that all was happening as he had foreseen it.

So Vader waited—and indeed, Luke and his fellow rebels did come to Endor. Vader sensed his son's presence on the forest moon. The moon was the site of a shield generator protecting the as-yet-unfinished Death Star. As the Emperor had predicted, there was no need to hunt the boy down—Luke surrendered to the Empire's troops in order to see Vader.

Luke admitted that he had come to accept that Vader was his father. But Luke also called him Anakin Skywalker, and urged him to reject the dark side.

Vader reacted angrily—Anakin was the name of his former self, a weak fool who had been betrayed and ruined. He was now Darth Vader, the Dark Lord of the Sith. But Luke insisted there was still good in his father, and told Vader he could feel the conflict within him. Vader told his son that it was too late—Vader had to obey his master, who would show Luke the true nature of the Force.

As ordered, Vader brought Luke to the Death Star and Sidious's throne room. There, Sidious tried to taunt

Luke into attacking him. He encouraged Luke to give into the anger and fear that would allow the dark side to conquer him. He informed Luke that his friends on the forest moon were walking into a trap, as was the rebel fleet that hoped to destroy the Death Star. To save the Rebel Alliance, Sidious said, Luke would have to take his lightsaber and strike Sidious down.

Luke refused, but as Vader watched, the rebel fleet arrived and was ambushed by the waiting Imperials—and by the Death Star, revealed as now fully operational. Everything Vader's son believed in was on the verge of being destroyed. And so, finally, the boy used the Force to summon his lightsaber and slash at the Emperor—only to have Vader intercept the attack with his own blade.

Father and son dueled again, and this time Luke knocked Vader off-balance. But Luke didn't press his advantage. He backed away, refusing to fight, and once again pleaded with his father to let go of his hate.

Vader used the Force to probe Luke's thoughts, and discovered a secret his son had been desperate to hide—Luke had a sister. Padmé had given birth to twins, both of whom were strong with the Force. If Luke wouldn't turn to the dark side, Vader told him, perhaps his sister Leia would.

The young Jedi responded to the threat against his sister with a desperate anger fueled by fear. He attacked and overwhelmed Vader. Luke knocked him to the floor with blows from his lightsaber and then hacked off Vader's mechanical hand.

Sidious, Vader's master, laughed with delight. Luke had surrendered to the dark side. Now, Sidious said, it was time for Luke to take his father's place by the Emperor's side.

Vader waited for his son to kill him. It was the way of the Sith for the strong to destroy the weak. Just as Anakin had replaced Dooku, Luke would replace Vader.

But Luke flung his lightsaber away and told Sidious that he had failed. Luke was a Jedi, like his father before him.

Sidious flew into a rage, blasting Luke with Force lightning as Vader struggled to his feet. Luke crumpled in pain. He was no match for the fury of the dark side. With the last of his strength, he begged his father to help him.

Vader knew his son would die. It was the price Luke would pay for his weakness. But was it weakness? Luke had shown him mercy. And even now, at the end, Luke believed there was good in his father—that Anakin Skywalker still lived somewhere within Darth Vader.

Vader gathered his strength and seized Sidious. Taken by surprise, the Emperor could do nothing. As Force lightning ripped through his own body, Vader hurled his master down a seemingly endless shaft into

the innards of the Death Star. Darth Sidious was dead—
and Anakin had fulfilled the destiny of the Chosen
One. He had once helped destroy the Jedi; now he had

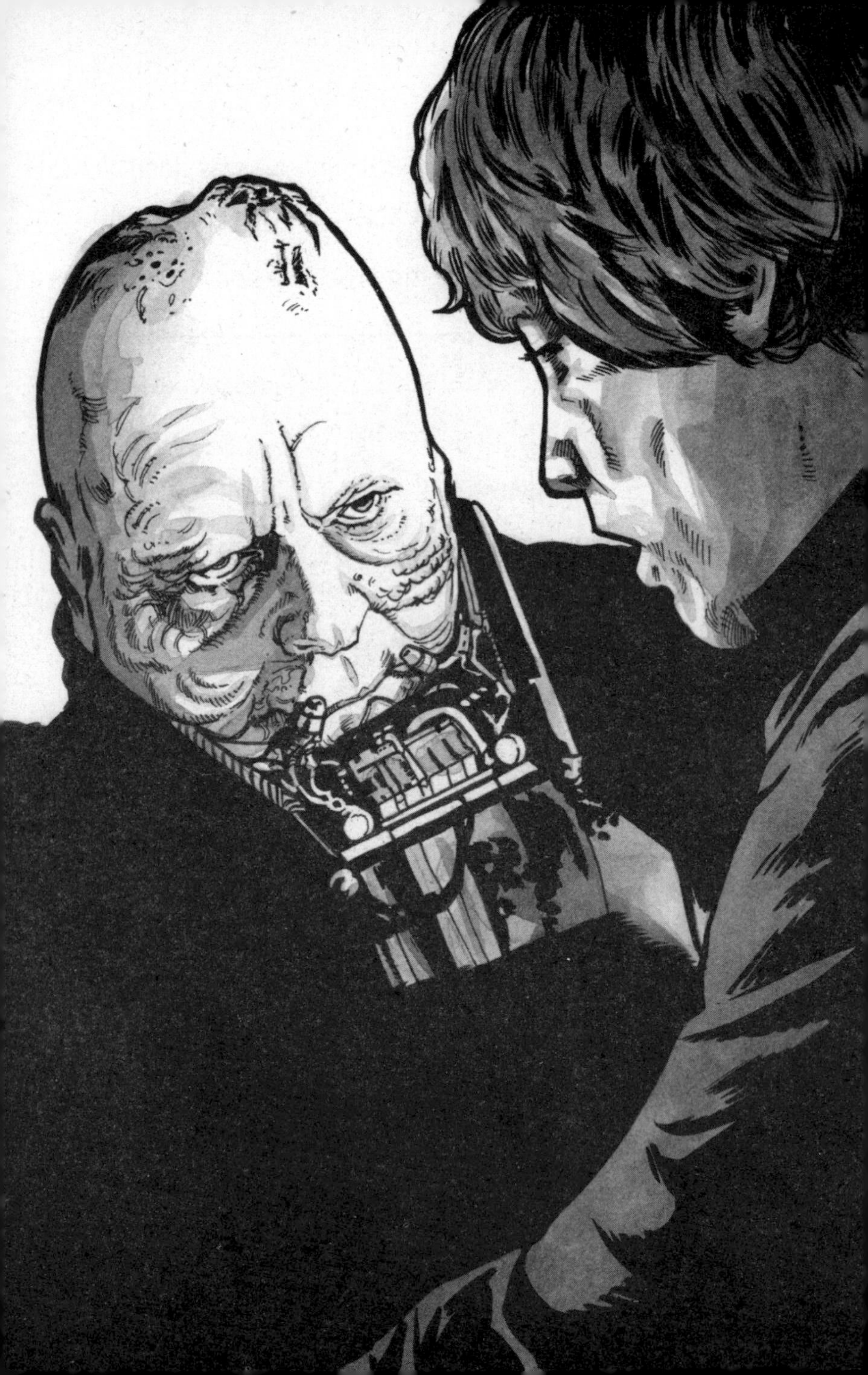

eliminated the Sith.

While rebel starfighters attacked the Death Star, Luke helped his father to a hangar and an Imperial shuttle. Vader knew he was dying, his body broken. He stopped Luke and asked his son to help him take off his mask, the only face the galaxy had known for decades. Anakin looked at his son with his own eyes, and managed to smile. "Tell your sister you were right," he said.

And then he died.

Luke returned to the forest moon of Endor and burned Vader's armor on a pyre, the flames reaching up to the stars in the night sky. He then returned to his friends and the rebel celebration. But, looking into the night, he saw a vision of three spectral figures glimmering in the darkness. He saw the Force spirits of Obi-Wan Kenobi and Yoda. And beside them stood Anakin, his body young and whole.

Darth Vader was dead. But Anakin Skywalker lived on in the Force.

Fast Facts

Anakin Skywalker had no father—his mother Shmi simply became pregnant. The Jedi Master Qui-Gon Jinn believed Anakin had been created by the Force itself, as foretold by the ancient prophecy of the Chosen One.

Anakin's ability to fly a podracer made people think he had superhuman reflexes, but the truth was a bit more complicated. Without knowing it, Anakin used the Force to see things before they happened, allowing him to anticipate events and take action more quickly than normal human beings could.

As Sith master and apprentice, Darth Sidious and Darth Vader constantly tested each other. This cruel tradition had kept the Sith strong during centuries of hiding. A weak master deserved to be overthrown, while a weak apprentice deserved to be replaced.

After Luke Skywalker discovered Darth Vader was his father, he believed that there was still good in him. He was right. Anakin eventually sacrificed himself to save his son and destroy Darth Sidious. This fulfilled the prophecy of the Chosen One.

⚙ Qui-Gon Jinn measured Anakin's midi-chlorian count—a measure of his potential ability with the Force—by taking a sample of his blood. The reading was over 20,000—higher than that of Yoda or any other Jedi.

⚙ Anakin used at least five lightsabers during his life. He built his first on Ilum as a Padawan, but it was cut in two in Geonosis's droid factory. He fought Count Dooku with two blades—both of which were replacement weapons brought by the Jedi when they rescued him and Obi-Wan. After his clash with Dooku, Anakin built a new lightsaber. Obi-Wan took that weapon after their duel on Mustafar and gave it to Luke Skywalker. As a Sith, Vader used a red-bladed lightsaber.

⚙ While trapped within the strange realm known as Mortis, Anakin had a Force vision of the evil he would do as Darth Vader. But the Force entity known as the Father erased the vision from his memory.

Glossary

apprentice: A person who studies and practices a skill with someone who has significant experience.

empire: A government that often has many territories under the rule of one leader, who is typically called an emperor.

Force: An energy field that surrounds, binds, and connects all living things.

galaxy: One of the many groups of stars that make up the universe.

hyperdrive: A state of very high activity; also a device that propels a ship or other vehicle to an extreme speed.

Imperial: A term for something related to an empire or emperor.

Jedi: A Force-sensitive individual who studies and utilizes the mystical energy of the Force.

Padawan: A Force-sensitive individual, often a teenager, who is training and studying with the Jedi Order.

Republic: A government where citizens elect officials.